The Life of Saint Douceline,
a Beguine of Provence

Library of Medieval Women ISSN 1369–9652

Series Editor: Jane Chance

The Library of Medieval Women aims to make available, in an English translation, significant works by, for, and about medieval women, from the age of the Church Fathers to the fifteenth century. The series encompasses many forms of writing, from poetry, visions, biography and autobiography, and letters, to sermons, treatises and encyclopedias; the subject matter is equally diverse: theology and mysticism, classical mythology, medicine and science, history, hagiography, and instructions for anchoresses. Each text is presented with an introduction setting the material in context, a guide to further reading, and an interpretive essay.

Already published

Christine de Pizan's Letter of Othea to Hector, *Jane Chance*, 1990

The Writings of Margaret of Oingt, Medieval Prioress and Mystic, *Renate Blumenfeld-Kosinski*, 1990

Saint Bride and her Book: Birgitta of Sweden's Revelations, *Julia Bolton Holloway*, 1992

The Memoirs of Helene Kottanner (1439–1440), *Maya Bijvoet Williamson*, 1998

The Writings of Teresa de Cartagena, *Dayle Seidenspinner-Núñez*, 1998

Julian of Norwich: *Revelations of Divine Love* and *The Motherhood of God*: an excerpt, *Frances Beer*, 1998

Hrotsvit of Gandersheim: A Florilegium of her Works, *Katharina M. Wilson*, 1998

Hildegard of Bingen: On Natural Philosophy and Medicine: Selections from *Cause et Cure, Margret Berger*, 1999

Women Saints' Lives in Old English Prose, *Leslie A. Donovan*, 1999

Angela of Foligno's Memorial, *Cristina Mazzoni*, 2000

The Letters of the Rožmberk Sisters, *John M. Klassen*, 2001

We welcome suggestions for future titles in the series. Proposals or queries may be sent directly to the editor or publisher at the addresses given below; all submissions will receive prompt and informed consideration.

Professor Jane Chance, Department of English, MS 30, Rice University, PO Box 1892, Houston, TX 77251–1892, USA. E-mail: jchance@rice.edu

Boydell & Brewer Limited, PO Box 9, Woodbridge, Suffolk, IP12 3DF, UK. E-mail: boydell@boydell.co.uk. Website: http://www.boydell.co.uk

The Life of Saint Douceline, a Beguine of Provence

Translated from the Occitan with Introduction, Notes and Interpretive Essay

Kathleen Garay
Madeleine Jeay
McMaster University

D.S. BREWER

First published 2001
Transferred to digital printing
Printed in paperback 2008
D.S. Brewer, Cambridge

ISBN 978-0-85991-629-5 Hardback
ISBN 978-1-84384-194-4 Paperback

D. S. Brewer is an imprint of Boydell & Brewer Ltd
PO Box 9, Woodbridge, Suffolk IP12 3DF, UK
and of Boydell & Brewer Inc.
668 Mt Hope Avenue, Rochester, NY 14620, USA
website: www.boydellandbrewer.com

A CiP catalogue record for this book is available
from the British Library

This publication is printed on acid-free paper

Contents

Acknowledgments

This edition, in its several years of gestation, has benefitted from the encouragement and assistance of many friends, students and colleagues at McMaster University; we are grateful to them all. We offer particular thanks to Dr Carol Kent for her excellent preliminary translation of the text. Madeleine Jeay expresses thanks for fruitful conversations with Dr Geneviève Brunel-Lobrichon, specialist in Occitan at the Sorbonne, and for insights and support from loved ones in Montreal. Kathy Garay is grateful to her daughters Amanda, Charlotte and Katherine, and her husband Nick for their unflagging encouragement and patience with her obsession. This mystic collaboration has been a great joy for us both. It has deepened our already close friendship and has led, in ever-widening circles, to a television series on women mystics (with another in preparation) and an interactive web-site on medieval women (http://www.mw.mcmaster.ca). We are delighted that the text, which started it all, is now ready for its readers.

Introduction

The object of this historical overview is to provide a context for the life of Douceline de Digne and for the vita which is presented here for the first time in English. In this introduction we will attempt to summarize the origins and development of the beguinal way of life, outline the process by which Douceline introduced this way of life to Provence, examine the manuscript of her vita and discuss its authorship. In the essay which follows this introduction we will proceed to address the unique aspects of the vita and present an analysis of this important and compelling text.

The Beguines in Medieval Europe

The life of Douceline (ca. 1215–74), founder of the Beguines of Marseilles, was written within the context of a Christendom-wide revival of popular religiosity, sparked by the Gregorian reform movement of the eleventh century. The resulting impulse towards a renewed spirituality, which found its most notable expression in new or reformed religious orders and a heightening of spiritual intensity among the laity, had particular significance for women. Saintly women like Hildegard of Bingen[1] and Elisabeth of Schönau in Germany found spiritual fulfillment and developed their visionary mysticism inside the traditional cloister. Hildegard undoubtedly contributed to the growing Cistercian interest in pious lay women[2] and she was particularly venerated by Philippe of Alsace, count of Flanders. Her visions and prophecies became a part of the spiritual heritage in Belgium. Although some new religious orders were established,[3] more and more women were to strive better to serve God without abandoning the world. During the twelfth century lay piety was encouraged and heightened by itinerant preachers whose main themes were the corruption in the Church and the need for

---

[1] McDonnell, 281.
[2] McDonnell, 286.
[3] The Premonstratensian Order, for example.

reform. Throughout Europe they were followed by crowds of people, among them many women.[4]

Emblematic of this new devotional intensity within which women would strive to find their place, was the development of the cult of St. Mary Magdalene.[5] After its development at Vezelay, her cult spread in Provence at the end of the twelfth and beginning of thirteenth century, promoted by wandering preachers. In 1225 the Congregation of the Penitents of St. Magdalene was established for female penitents[6] and one of the cult's most persuasive supporters was Robert of Arbrissel, founder of a convent at Fontevrault.[7] Salimbene describes the shrine at Sainte-Baume after his visit in 1248 and Joinville recounts the visit of the saintly king, Louis IX, in July 1254.[8] The Magdalene's popularity seems to have stemmed from the fact that she represented the common sinner – a fallible everyman and everywoman – not an inaccessible ideal of perfection like the Virgin Mary. As a model of repentance, she embodied the possibility of forgiveness and redemption, and a number of female mystics were profoundly influenced by her.[9]

*

Despite considerable scholarly attention, the early history of the development of the beguine way of life for women, like that of their male counterparts, the beghards, remains largely obscure. It is likely that, as Ernest McDonnell has suggested,[10] it was a spontaneous movement which recognized no single founder. However, its ideological roots are clear enough; they can be traced from the widespread attempt to address the question of "whether each and every Christian might not be called by the command of the gospels and the example

---

4   Robert of Arbrissel, for example, who founded a convent at Fontevrault and Norbert of Xanten who established his order at Prémontré: Murk-Jansen 1998, 19–20; Bolton 1976, 142.
5   Brunel-Lobrichon 1988a, 42; Ludwig-Jansen mentions that the resurgence of her cult in the twelfth century lasted for 500 years (1998, 67) and that late medieval preachers accepted her role in the redemption drama. Also Muessig (in Kienzle and Walker, 146) argues that the legend of Mary Magdalene provides an example of a woman preaching, as does the legend of Catherine of Alexandria.
6   Saxer, 221–23.
7   Saxer, 107–25.
8   Joinville, 330–31.
9   Haskins, 177–79, Ludwig-Jansen 2000. Examples include mystic women as different as Elisabeth of Schönau (Clark, 53) and Margery Kempe.
10 McDonnell, 5.

of the apostles to model his or her life on the gospels and apostolic standards".[11] This movement, promoting a return to evangelical authenticity,[12] was supported and disseminated by the vernacular preaching which was at the heart of the general movement towards the popularization of religion. Such popular preachers as Lambert le Bègue who, in the late 1170s, promoted clerical reform in the diocese of Liège and translated portions of the Bible for the edification of laymen, were apostles of the new popular religious movement.[13] This burgeoning lay spirituality was closely related to the rise of urbanization and its most well-developed effects can be seen in areas where urban development was most pronounced.

In some areas monastic houses, unable or unwilling to accommodate more women, began to turn away new recruits, just at the time when women of the new urban classes were seeking some form of communal spirituality. The proliferation of new foundations of nunneries was insufficient for the ever-increasing number of pious women, intent on adopting lives of devotion and poverty, especially in the diocese of Liège.[14] But this practical difficulty was compounded by the ambiguous attitude of the male orders: the Premonstratensians and Cistercians were reluctant to assume either pastoral or economic responsibility for the women and were anxious to exclude them from their abbeys,[15] while women continued to be disadvantaged by not being allowed to regulate their own forms of religious life and to found their own independent orders.[16]

There is evidence that pious women in the north were first attracted to the Premonstratensian order. When the order refused to accept more recruits they joined the Cistercians; when they too refused to take any more "these women formed communities belonging to no order at all, following no specific rule, but binding themselves in all strictness to commandments of female piety in chastity and poverty, prayer and fasting".[17] By the early thirteenth century the emergence of the Franciscan and Dominican orders in

11 Grundmann, 7.
12 Brunel-Lobrichon 1997, 163.
13 McDonnell, 71–72.
14 McDonnell, 116–19; Murk-Jansen 1998, 21.
15 The general chapter of the Cistercians in 1213 limited the number of nunneries, and then, in 1228, forbade further attachment of nunneries to the order: Bolton 1976, 143.
16 Bolton 1976, 143, 154.
17 McDonnell, 78.

Southern Europe provided new spiritual opportunities for men, but for their female would-be followers the mendicant lifestyle was not a practical possibility. Moreover, both of the male mendicant orders strenuously resisted the women's claims on their ministry and their resources.[18]

Yet while some women may have been thwarted in their efforts to join established orders, others may well have found the life of a beguine, one who lived a spiritual life while continuing to live and work in the world, a more satisfying way of emulating the apostolic life.[19] It is clear that many of the communities of *humiliati* in Italy, as well as groups of *mulieres religiosae* in southern Flanders, predate the establishment of the Franciscan order. This new form of religious practice was to spread beyond Italy and Flanders and was develop a vigorous identity and momentum of its own.

The beguine's way of life can be seen as "semi-religious", situated liminally between the formal religious life of a nun and the life of a lay woman. The beguinage was a retreat, especially well adapted to an urban society, where women living in common could pursue a spiritual life. Rather than being tied for life to a formal vow of poverty, chastity and obedience, the beguine's obligation to observe chastity and obedience was considered temporary in nature, conditioned by personal desire and contingent on residence in the beguinage. Simple vows, often made without witnesses, distinguished the induction of a beguine from the public profession made by a nun.[20] As we shall see in Douceline's vita, the question of poverty was a complex one but, in general, beguines could retain their property or even acquire property while living in the community.[21]

Members of the beguinage might engage in weaving, carding,

---

[18] See Grundmann's discussion of the response to Clare and her followers, 64; also Bolton 1976, 151–53.

[19] Clare's struggles to win acceptance for her own Rule make clear how problematic for the Church establishment was the concept of women who were not firmly enclosed. For example, Grundmann cites the papal bull of 1241, ordering all archbishops and bishops "to act against women moving about barefoot, belted with rope, dressed in the habit of the Order of St. Damian". These women, described as *religio simulata*, were clearly not genuine, since the real order was bound by rules of strict enclosure (Grundmann, 115).

[20] McDonnell, 130–31.

[21] McDonnell, 146–49.

sewing or educating children[22] as well as charitable work.[23]
"Following the principle of economic and practical self-mainte-
nance, Beguines worked for and supported one another by the
income of personal dowries, carding wool, or washing laundry
locally."[24] The urban environment was an essential component of this
new model of female piety. It both justified and made possible their
lives of community service and it marked the evolution from the
earlier era in which women's religious experience was primarily
identified with powerful aristocratic abbesses and canonesses in
enclosed environments. Anticipating Francis's instruction to be "in
the world but not of the world", beguine communities attracted
women from the newly emerging patriciate[25] but in some areas they
also included poorer women, looking for material sustenance as well
as a life of devotion.[26] While the material possessions of its members
helped to sustain the community, such wealth often brought with it a
sense of anxiety because of its potential to undermine the ideal of
poverty.[27]

Phillipen's studies of the beguines in southern Flanders[28] have
suggested that there were four stages in the evolution to the large
begijnhof or beguine parish: holy women living separately or under
the parental roof, without abandoning either their trade or the possibility of marriage; women living in communities under a leader,
often emulating convent life in their organization and daily practices;
enclosed communities, the *beguinae clausae*, and, finally, the
beguinage large enough to form an autonomous parish. The last two
stages seem only to have been achieved in significant numbers in
Flanders and Walloon Belgium. In her work on the same area in the
thirteenth century, Ziegler observes only two main forms: the
convent beguinage in which women "lived together in small, isolated
communities scattered about the town or under the parental roof,
usually numbering but a handful of women, at most, in any given

---

22 Beatrice of Nazareth was sent at the age of seven to live with a group of beguines in
a nearby town "that she might make progress in virtue." (De Gank, 25).
23 McDonnell, 146.
24 Ziegler, 1992, 73.
25 McDonnell, 82.
26 Ziegler, 1992, 71. According to Schmitt, there is was sociological evolution from
beguinages which consisted largely of the urban patriciate in the thirteenth century
to houses which functioned as refuges for poor women in the fourteenth and fifteenth centuries (19).
27 McDonnell, 97–97.
28 The work of L.J.M. Phillipen, cited by McDonnell, 5.

house" and, existing at precisely the same time, "large, all-female housing settlements, known as *curtis* beguinages".[29] Beguines in Germany, with its multiplicity of small convents, seem to have lived primarily according to the convent model or Phillipen's first and second stages. While the structural aspects of the beguine phenomenon in France await further study, the movement's development appears closer to the German than to the Flemish model, and Douceline's houses in Hyères and Marseilles can be confidently placed at the second level of development.

The reaction of the church establishment to these beguine communities was cautious at best. While Innocent III's Fourth Lateran Council forbade the establishment of new religious orders in 1215, he did not move specifically against the beguines, indeed Grundmann suggests that he "opened the way for the religious movement to join the Church and work within the limits of the Catholic hierarchy".[30] The day after Innocent's death, on 16 July 1216, Jacques de Vitry,[31] the supporter and biographer of the holy women of Liège, appeared at the curia. He won oral approval from Honorius III for the pious women of Liège and all of Belgium, France and Germany, to live together in communal houses and to form female cloistered communities without accepting any approved rule. Douceline's two communities were to initially flourish within the context of this approval. Further bulls assuring the recognition of groups of beguines followed[32] and this ecclesiastical support was complemented by the protection of local rulers or royal patronage.[33]

Jacques de Vitry, an Augustinian canon, born into a noble family at Vitry-sur-Seine, was lured from his studies in Paris by accounts of the sanctity of Marie of Oignies, the woman who was at the centre of the new religious movement in the diocese of Liège. Vitry became her confessor and wrote her life, presenting Marie as the prototype of the beguine life.[34] After Marie's death in 1213, Vitry preached the crusade against the Albigensian heretics of southern France, and he

---

[29] Ziegler, 1992, 70.

[30] Grundmann, 78.

[31] Circa 1170–1240.

[32] For example, on 30 May 1233 the bull *Gloriam virginalem* of Pope Gregory IX recognized the Belgian beguines, and those of the diocese of Cologne had their privileges secured by papal legates in 1228–31: McDonnell, 157–65; and for the succession of privileges granted to different beguinages, see McDonnell, 176–85.

[33] McDonnell, 205–18; 226–40.

[34] McDonnell, 7.

recounts that he wrote her biography, in part, to provide a model "contemporary saint" to serve as an example for the southern French heretics.[35] McNamara has demonstrated how the growth of heresy was paralleled by this "women's movement" in Flanders, Italy and southern France, dedicated to the defence of orthodoxy. There was an alliance between the men engaged in extirpating heresy, particularly the Dominicans,[36] and those women whose mystical revelations validated their teachings.[37] The Dominican Thomas de Cantimpré, an admirer and disciple of Vitry, was also to heed the call to "gather up the fragments lest they be lost".[38] As well as a supplement to the life of Marie (written ca. 1230), Cantimpré wrote the vitae of Christine of Saint-Trond (1224), Margaret of Ypres (1240) and Lutgard of Aywières (ca. 1248).[39] Cantimpré's vitae were all composed during the life of Douceline de Digne.

Douceline was born shortly after the death of Marie d'Oignies, in 1215 or 1216, to a wealthy family, likely in the town of Digne in Provence, in the south of France. Her father, a wealthy merchant called Bérenguier (or Bérenger), was from Digne, and her mother, Hugue, was from Barjols where the family lived when Douceline was a child. When her mother died around 1230, Douceline moved to Hyères with her father, probably to be closer to her brother Hugh who was a member of the town's Franciscan monastery. Hugh was to become a well-known Franciscan theologian and preacher and was to have a significant role in assisting Douceline with her life's mission. A second brother died young leaving two daughters, Douceline and Marie, who later followed their aunt's way of life.[40]

Just as communities of devout women gathered around Marie at Oignies and Nivelles and around Lutgard at Aywières in the diocese of Liège, so they were to gather around Douceline at Hyères and Marseilles. After a very pious childhood and teenage years which were devoted to the care of the poor and sick in her father's house, she experienced a "conversion" at the age of 20 and, several years afterwards, took vows before her brother Hugh and established her first beguine community near the Roubaud River on the edge of the

35 Jacques de Vitry, 48; Vauchez 1987b.
36 But also the Franciscans, especially in the south.
37 McNamara 1993 in Wiethaus, 9.
38 Jacques de Vitry, 39.
39 See the introduction to the *Supplement to the Life of Marie D'Oignies*, Thomas de Cantimpré 1999a, 204.
40 Albanés, xl–xliii.

town of Hyères (ca. 1241). She subsequently founded a second house
in the town of Hyères itself, closer to the Franciscans, whose church
she and her ladies attended.[41] Then, around 1250, she established
another community on the outskirts of Marseilles. Douceline lived in
the Marseilles house and continued as leader of the communities in
both towns until her death in 1274.

At the time she settled there, Marseilles was a thriving port city,
formerly under the titular control of Raymond-Berengar IV, the count
of Provence, but in fact dominated by an oligarchy of wealthy
merchants who continued vigorously to defend their privileges from
a growing population of workers, sailors and artisans.[42] In 1246
Charles of Anjou, youngest brother of King Louis IX, obtained the
County of Provence through his marriage to Count Raymond's
heiress, Beatrice, and he lost no time in claiming his rights over the
city. The city repulsed his first attack in August 1251 but sued for
peace the following year; there was unrest and resistance to the new
regime until 1256 when a treaty was signed which allowed Marseilles
to keep its judicial and fiscal autonomy but which surrendered all
political power to the Count. Both the city's wide class divisions and
its state of political unrest made it an ideal place for Douceline's new
foundation: the large numbers of poor and marginalized provided the
clientele for nursing care and the dispensing of charity, while the
contentious urban patriciate provided an ideal audience for Franciscan preaching as well as a potential source of support, both political and financial.[43]

Douceline's uncompromising adoption of the term "beguine" for
herself and the women of her community, as described in the vita,
indicates her awareness of some of the troubled history of the word:
"she would say that the name of Beguine pleased her greatly and that
she held it in great esteem because it was humble and scorned by the
world's pride" (4:2). The word – and hence the movement – had
acquired an association with heresy.[44] According to Grundmann, the

---

[41] Albanés, xlv. The first house at Roubaud seems to have been closed at about this
time; by the time of the fall of Antioch in 1260 there was clearly only one house in
Hyères.
[42] Baratier 1973b, 84–88, Runciman, 88–91.
[43] The political support of Charles of Anjou and his wife Beatrice is evident throughout Douceline's Life, and at the end of the vita we find a reference to the generous
financial support of the citizens, when her body was translated to the sumptuous
new church of the Franciscans and placed in a rich marble tomb, 14:36.
[44] Grundmann, 80.

entire women's spiritual movement in the district of Liège had been under a cloud of suspicion until Jacques de Vitry won them recognition from the papal curia and suspicious officials had called them "beguines", the same name they used for the Cathar heretics of southern France.[45] Like the universal church itself, religious women of the period often had international connections.[46] Douceline had the additional advantage of access to official channels through her brother Hugh. It is therefore probable that she knew exactly what she was doing in adopting the name of beguine for her ladies.

While attitudes to the term "beguine" and the movement it connoted seem to have been gradually changing following Vitry's successful intervention,[47] the ecclesiastical authorities continued to be concerned about the multiplication of extra-regular communities and particularly what was considered the unstable and potentially troubling form of life of women who took the vow of chastity and adopted a particular habit without entering a convent.[48] Although they were not the main target, beguines were involved in a mid-thirteenth-century dispute[49] between the leaders of the University of Paris, including William of St. Amour, and the mendicant orders, over the increasing role played by the mendicants in academic life. In their efforts to discredit the friars, the secular masters also aimed at the beguines because of the women's association with the mendicants and their shared choice of a life of evangelical poverty while being in the world. In the works of important authors such as Jean de Meun and Rutebeuf, beguines became a symbol of hypocrisy.[50] Once the Cathar heresy had been eradicated, the formation of groups of semi-religious women and their involvement in the pastoral care of the faithful became less and less accepted. The history of the beguine movement for the next two centuries sees it regularly falling under

---

45 Grundmann, 80. The etymology of the word itself is contested, *The Catholic Encyclopedia* (New York, 1907) suggests a derivation from the old Flemish word *beghen* meaning "to pray" (see Beguines and Beghards, Vol. II, 389–90).

46 Hadewich of Brabant, for example, who probably lived among the beguines of Nivelles in Flanders, was in contact with a female hermit in Saxony, and she knew of like-minded women in Thuringia, Bohemia, England and Paris (Grundmann, 80).

47 The records of the city of Cologne apply the term simply to lay religious women as early as 1223, and Grundmann suggests that, at least according to the German evidence, by 1245 the word had lost all hint of heresy (80).

48 McDonnell, 95.

49 1253–58.

50 Moorman 125–31; Congar.

suspicion and being linked with heresy.[51] The beguine Marguerite Porete was burned in Paris in 1310[52] and religious women were burned in the Rhineland and southern France in 1318 and 1328 by Dominican inquisitors, among them Bernard Gui.[53] The movement was then caught in the struggle against the "heresy of the Free Spirit", also known as the "Beguine heresy". The fifteenth century was a time during which the ecclesiastical authorities increased their control over all forms of lay piety, with figures like Jean Gerson criticizing religious women, and Dominican inquisitors brandishing the threat of witchcraft.

However, during the thirteenth century, before the development of this ecclesiastical "backlash", pious women managed to find a space and to have their contribution recognized by the church authorities. Apart from the support the movement had won from the pope and influential church officials, and the saintly reputations of the northern beguines, the movement seems to have gradually gained wider acceptance by narrowing its focus to strict adherence to the ideals of poverty and chastity, distinguishing itself from heretical movements by abandoning apostolic activity and avoiding any public demands that the clergy and Church conform more closely to the apostolic model.[54] Using Saint Francis as her model – he died in 1226 when she was about ten years old – Douceline emulated his life, espousing not only his lack of possessions but his determined flight from wealth, refusing to call anything her own.[55] Her community was to consist primarily of educated women from upper-class or even noble families, but Douceline did not expect the same rigorous poverty of them; instead they were allowed to dedicate their wealth to the sustenance and stability of the community (5:11).

As will be further discussed below, Douceline was well connected and her social stature, as well as her saintly reputation and spiritual powers, not only assisted in ensuring the survival of her own founda-

---

[51] Pope John XXII issued bulls condemning "women who call themselves beguines" (Grundmann, 185).

[52] Grundmann, 183.

[53] McNamara 1993 in Wiethaus 1993, 22.

[54] Marguerite Porete's proselytizing and her book *The Mirror of Simple Souls*, with its clear criticism of the clergy and the Church, violated these constraints and hence she was burned in Paris in 1310.

[55] Compare Douceline with the northern "model" beguine, Marie d'Oignies. Marie was the daughter of wealthy parents, who was compelled to marry at the age of 14 and who soon persuaded her husband to live chastely and give away their wealth to poor.

tions at Hyères and Marseilles but also, indirectly, contributed to the spread of the beguine movement throughout France. Her brother Hugh's status as a compelling and influential preacher is recorded in both Salimbene's chronicle[56] and Joinville's *Life of St. Louis*. Hugh was asked to preach by the king in July 1254 at Hyères[57] and he was in contact with some of the most learned figures of the time, such as Robert Grosseteste, whom he certainly met at the Council of Lyons in 1235 and with whom he exchanged an erudite correspondence.[58] After Hugh's death ca. 1255–56, Douceline received support and spiritual care from John of Parma and Jaucelin. John had just been elected Minister General of the Franciscans,[59] an office he held for ten years. Jaucelin was first provincial minister of the Franciscans,[60] then Bishop of Orange,[61] and he assisted Douceline until her death when he gave her eulogy.[62]

Nor were Douceline's connections limited to powerful ecclesiastical figures. Many of the women who followed her into the beguine way of life and entered her community belonged to the most important and powerful aristocratic families of Provence, among them Philippine Porcellet, the woman who is assumed to be the author of her Life. Also, as we shall see, one of the most crucial relationships for Douceline herself and her community was the one she developed with Charles of Anjou and his wife Beatrice, count and the countess of Provence. Because of her success in securing the safe birth of their baby girl, Douceline became the godmother of the child and thenceforth enjoyed the couple's full support.[63] It seems likely that the favour and trust of Charles of Anjou, brother of the king, Louis IX, contributed to royal support for the movement.[64] Louis became an enthusiastic and generous supporter of the beguines throughout France. The Paris house, near the gate of Barbeel,[65] established sometime before November 1264, was built on a large tract of land in order to accommodate the multitude of "honestarum mulierum, quae

---

56 Salimbene, 216–31.
57 Joinville, 326–48.
58 Salimbene (225) also mentions brother Adam March, himself a great scholar, among his friends; Brunel-Lobrichon 1988a, 45.
59 1247.
60 1262.
61 1272.
62 Albanés, lvii; Gout, 281.
63 Circa 1255 according to Albanés, xlvii.
64 Louis was married to Beatrice's sister, Margaret – see Runciman, 88.
65 McDonnell, 224.

beguinae communiter appellantur".[66] Although, as we have seen, negative attitudes towards the beguines continued and were to intensify in subsequent centuries, Douceline's friends in high places ensured that her houses were protected. Troubles were to multiply after her death; the Hyères house closed and the Marseilles community suffered from the war in Provence in 1357 and 1361, which forced the sisters to take refuge inside the walls of the town. The house lasted until 1407 when the last prioress, Marguerite d'Alon, donated it to the Franciscans who took possession of it after her death in 1414.[67]

Douceline's political role had repercussions beyond the history of her own order; she was intimately involved in the development of the Franciscan Order in southern France and in the difficulties it encountered. The order came to Provence as early as 1217 with the mission of John Bonelli.[68] Her brother Hugh, a major figure of the order, was a recognized member of the Spiritual fringe, a group which refused to compromise the original ideal of evangelical simplicity and poverty. Hugh has been called "the father of Spirituals"[69] and Douceline's other spiritual guide, John of Parma, followed the same orientation. During Douceline's lifetime relations between the Spirituals and the Conventuals became progressively more confrontational. One issue dividing the two groups, one which had repercussions in the context of Douceline's life, concerned their differing attitudes to the apocalyptic works of Joachim of Fiore. Hugh's own interest in Joachimism could have made him suspect, but he died before the crisis which occurred following the circulation of Brother Gerard of Borgo San Donnino's *Liber introductorius ad Evangeliam Eternum* in 1254. Gerard announced the immediate advent of the Third Age of the Holy Ghost. The book and its author were condemned for heresy, and the dispute contributed to the conflict between the seculars and the mendicants at the University of Paris.[70] In the wake of this conflict, John of Parma himself came under attack when the conventuals, wanting to be rid of this promoter of strict observance, targeted his weak point, his admiration for

66 *Beati Ludovici Vita*, cited McDonnell, 225.
67 Albanés, lxxi–lxxii.
68 Moorman 65; in 1219 Christopher of Cahors was appointed as first Provincial Minister. The first settlements were in Mirepoix, Arles, Aix, Montpellier, and in 1222 houses were established in Draguignan, Nîmes and Apt; Baratier 1973a.
69 Moorman, 189.
70 Moorman, 128–46; Reeves 1969, 60–63.

Joachim of Fiore. He was forced to resign as Minister General of the Order in 1257 and was replaced by St. Bonaventure.[71]

The existence of groups of lay religious men and women in southern France other than those who gathered around Douceline's leadership, is closely related to these two interconnected issues, the conflict between Spirituals and Conventuals, and the identification of the former with Joachimism. Already during Hugh's life, Salimbene recounts how

> There were a large number of notaries, judges, physicians, and learned men there who, on solemn feats days, would gather in Brother Hugh's chambers to hear him speak on the doctrine of Joachim, teaching and expounding the mysteries of Holy Scripture and predicting the future.[72]

Daniel[73] attributes the northward shift of Joachimism from Hyères to Paris to the activities of this group; it was also spread by Hugh's successor as a leader for lay religious people and fellow Joachimite, Peter John Olivi.[74] Among Olivi's followers who were accused and punished by the inquisitor Bernard Gui, was Prous Boneta, who received revelations at Olivi's tomb and in the church of the Franciscans in Marseilles.[75] The Roubaud community itself also suffered from the Church establishment's discomfort regarding semi-religious groups. When the decree of the Council of Vienne in 1311 suppressed convents of beguines and beghards, the order was temporarily dissolved, until in 1320, 1323 and 1325 three bulls exonerated Douceline's followers.[76] Continued repression did not stop the movement's spread from Provence to Gascony and to Toulouse and its environs,[77] where, at the end of the fourteenth century, Constance de Rabastens received apocalyptic visions.[78] This support of southern French beguins and beguines for the Spiritual Franciscans and the Joachimite views of their most influential leaders constitutes a significant difference between them and the northern beguines.

---

71 Salimbene 224 and 230–31; Moorman 102–14; Reeves 1969, 186–87.

72 Salimbene, 227.

73 Daniel, 148.

74 Olivi began preaching and teaching in Montpellier in 1289 (Manselli 1976 and 1989).

75 Burr 1985, 287–88; Manselli 1989, 34–37 and 196. See essay below, 148, notes 108–15.

76 Included by Albanés in his edition of *La Vie de Sainte Douceline* as Pièces Justificatives, 276, 277, 299. We are following Manselli in using the French term beguin rather than the northern beghard for the male groups.

77 Manselli 1989, 214–17.

After Douceline's death, Jaucelin presided over the translation of her corpse into a monument erected in the Franciscan church, and then, on 17 October 1278, she was moved once again, this time into the new church, where she was placed near her brother.[79] A cult began to develop which was never sanctioned by formal canonization. The last part of her Life details the many miracles she performed both before and after her death. Funds were allocated for having a lamp continually burning at her tomb; her feast was celebrated on 1 September in Hyères and Marseilles, and she may even have had an office composed in her honour.[80] The memory of Douceline is still very much alive in Hyères where the St. Douceline church has been erected in honour of Douceline and St. Louis, and a book about her is available for the information of parishioners and visitors. After more than 800 years the holy mother still inspires prayers and supplications.

The Manuscript – physical characteristics and history

Li vida de la benaurada sancta Doucelina has survived in a single, unique manuscript, presently housed in the Bibliothèque Nationale in Paris, fonds français 13503. Written on vellum, the small volume measures 16.7 x 12 cm and is made up of ten sections, each of ten leaves, with a final gathering of four leaves at the end. The text of the Life, written in a single fourteenth-century hand, is completed at folio 102; the verso of the penultimate leaf, folio 103, contains the formula for professing a member of the order of beguines and a hymn, both written in a later, but still fourteenth-century, hand. Brunel-Lobrichon supports Albanés's hypothesis that the manuscript corresponds to a second version of the Life dating from ca. 1315.[81] The neatly written manuscript lacks ornamentation, except for the chapter headings which are written in red, a single capital letter, ornamented in red and blue, at the opening of the manuscript and at the beginning of each chapter, and a blue and red border which is used on three sides of the first page and in the interior or exterior margins of subsequent pages at the start of chapters. Albanés suggests that the scribe was the man whose name appears at the end

---

78 See Hiver-Bérenguier.

79 Albanés, lvii–lviii.

80 Albanés, lviii–lxix: funding was provided for the celebration of her feast until 1407.

of the manuscript as Jacques le Pécheur,[82] about whom we know no more.

There is no doubt that the manuscript originated in Marseilles; this was the only area where the cult of Douceline developed and the later addition of the formula for the profession of the sisters refers to the sisters of Marseilles.[83] The history of the volume, carefully reconstructed by Albanés,[84] clearly indicates that the manuscript was not originally owned by the beguine community but rather was the property of one Cécile de la Voute, a beguine of Roubaud, who left it to her heirs and then, upon their deaths, instructed that it be returned to the community at Roubaud.[85] When the house was closed in 1414 it is probable that the manuscript, along with the rest of the order's possessions, came into the custody of the Friars Minor of Marseilles until that house was destroyed during the siege of the city in 1524 and the Franciscans were relocated to the cathedral. By the seventeenth century the *vida* appears in the library of Louis Charles de Valois, Count of Auvergne and natural son of Charles IX who inherited his father's library,[86] and from there Albanés has traced it to a Minorite community in Burgundy, where Louis Charles was buried.[87] With the closing of the convent during the Revolution, its books were dispersed and the manuscript made its way to a new owner; its provenance is noted on the volume: "Livre de la bibliothèque de Philibert Bouché, de Cluny". Somewhere between 1815 and 1830 it arrived at its final destination, the Bibliothèque Nationale.[88]

The Life of St. Douceline – authorship
The life of Saint Douceline belongs to that flowering of Lives written in the wake of the heretic movements and in reaction against them, directed towards the edification of the laity, especially women. What distinguishes Douceline's Life from most of those written about women mystics is the fact that it is not the product of a male authorship or the result of a collaboration with a male spiritual partner.[89]

---

81 1988a, 42.
82 Life of Saint Douceline, 16:33.
83 Albanés, Pièces Justificatives, 257.
84 Albanés, xiv–xvii.
85 Albanés, xiv.
86 Albanés, xv.
87 Albanés, xvi.
88 Albanés, xvii.

The conclusions of its first modern editor and translator into French, Abbot Albanés, have been corroborated by a more recent editor, R. Gout. The project of gathering information about the mystical journey of their founder and delivering her message through her biography must have emanated from the sisters themselves, who had an earlier version of the work read to them for the first time at the celebration of Douceline's feast on 1 September 1297.[90] The most obvious indication of its authorship is the fact that the Life did not borrow the language of the learned and clerics, Latin. Rather, it was written in the vernacular Provençal. Also, as Albanés notes, no outsider could have described the location so precisely – the oratory, dormitory and garden – or known in such accurate detail the circumstances of the events recounted or been able to so often quote Douceline's own words. A reliable sign that the author of the Life belonged to the community of beguines is her unquestioning enthusiasm for the saint and her deep admiration for the institution, which is said to be under the protection of God and the Holy Trinity.[91] At one point in the narrative, the author almost reveals her identity as one of the saint's "children" (14:32).[92]

Albanés' identification of Philippine Porcellet as the author of the Life, among all the sisters who belonged to the important aristocratic houses of the region, is entirely convincing.[93] Her entry into the community is described in some detail in the Life because it affords the opportunity to reveal Douceline's commitment to poverty; the holy mother declines Philippine's offer to donate her wealth.[94] This young widow, the mother of three daughters, was related to one of the most rich and powerful families of Provence.[95] Her brother,

---

[89] It is not, however, a unique case, other examples being the Lives of Beatrice of Ornacieu by Marguerite d'Oingt and of Margaret of Colonna by an unnamed companion. Goodich, 55–59, also mentions a few autobiographies.

[90] Albanés, xxiii–xxv.

[91] Albanés, xxvii–xxviii: the institution is often referred to as "aquel sant estamen", this holy establishment; the name "beguine" is considered as a "holy" name.

[92] Albanés also notes the occurrence of "we" in several places (xxix).

[93] Albanés, xxx–xxxiii.

[94] Albanés, 43.

[95] See Aurell, 165–69 and Gout, 11, for details on Philippine's well-connected family and her biography before she joined Roubaud. Her father, Bertrand de Porcellet, was buried in the church of the knights of St. John of Jerusalem. She was the widow of Fouques d'Agout de Pontevès and mother of three daughters. The death of her husband must have occurred early in her life because she survived Douceline by more than 40 years (Albanés, xxxi).

Guillaume Porcellet, was a counsellor of Charles of Anjou, king of Sicily, the only Frenchman who was not killed in the massacre of the Sicilian Vespers. Philippine's wealth was to prove useful to the community, as when she acquired properties surrounding the beguines' house in Marseilles.[96] But her most significant contribution must have been her spiritual stature, recognized by Douceline herself, who designated her as the prioress to whom she would submit and whom she would obey.[97] After Douceline's death, Philippine was elected as the prioress of the convent and she held that office when the first version of the Life was written and read for the celebration of the founder's feast.

Because it was composed by a sister who was a member of the community, the text faithfully reflects the ideals and intentions of the beguines themselves. An indication of its importance for them is demonstrated by two miracles, one connected with its writing and another with its public reading. During the writing of the Life, one of the sisters began to have doubts about referring to Douceline as a saint.[98] One night, Douceline appeared to a novice who was stricken by a sudden illness; she touched the novice's feet with her hand so that the sick sister was totally healed, then she showed herself to the doubting sister, who repented of her evil thoughts. This anecdote provides an illustration of all the sisters' involvement in the gathering and selection of data for the composition of the Life. The second miracle occurred the very day of the first reading of Douceline's Life when Maragde Porcellet, Philippine's niece, was cured of her loss of the power of speech.[99] Both stories stress the text's importance for the whole community, which was its primary audience. The purpose of the Life, beyond its role as spiritual model for the sisters, was clearly to promote the idea of Douceline's saintliness and to provide grounds for her canonization, a crucial element in ensuring the community's survival. Within the houses themselves, Douceline's Life and example were meant to reinforce the sisters' sense of mission and identification to a common spiritual approach. Outside, the recognition of Douceline as a saint would strengthen the position of her institution in the eyes of the Church hierarchy, especially in the

96 Albanés, Pièces Justificatives, 265–68, 289–91.
97 According to Albanés' hypothesis (xxxiii).
98 Albanés, 203.
99 Albanés, 235.

context of the 1311 Concilliar decrees that had forced the Roubaud houses to be dismantled.[100]

This image of the Life of a spiritual woman, conceived, written and promoted by the group of women around her, primarily for their own purposes, contrasts with other lives, many of which were written as the result of a male partnership, usually with the confessor and spiritual advisor of the mystic. It is instructive to compare the matter of authorship, as well as other aspects of the experience of Douceline and her group of beguines, with the almost contemporary lay mystics of Flanders whose lives were written by Jacques de Vitry and Thomas de Cantimpré.[101]

As the first group of pious lay women to be presented as models of saintly lives, Christina the Astonishing, Margaret of Ypres, Marie d'Oignies and Yvette of Huy are the appropriate parallel to southern French beguines. The Life of the nun Lutgard of Aywières also belongs to the same group of women who knew and interacted with each other. For all of them, the progress of their lives was driven by the ideal of sainthood.[102]

In considering the Lives of Belgian beguines themselves, we must also consider their authors' personalities and goals. Jacques de Vitry was seminal in the recognition by the pope in 1216 of the legitimacy of groups of spiritual lay women living together.[103] He acted as an advisor and partner for devout women such as Lutgard of Aywières and Marie d'Oignies, receiving his inspiration from them as well as

---

[100] On the impact of these biographies, Lauwers (83) contradicts Vauchez (1991, 30) who considers it limited.

[101] Our methodological approach combines in-depth analysis of particular lives, such as Douceline's, with references to a large corpus of biographies in order to validate generalizations. About the importance of this pious lay movement: Vauchez 1991, 29. On groups of beguines elsewhere than in Belgium, see Galloway and McDonnell.

[102] Selecting sources only from canonized saints is too restrictive: the perspective of the godly woman and her biographer is in each case determined by an ideal of sainthood rather than the intention to give a real account of beguine spirituality (Lauwers). See Goodich who includes non-canonization documents. The biography of Dauphine de Puimichel also provides an interesting perspective even if she lived several generations after Douceline. Like her, she represents southern French lay spirituality, developed and channelled through Franciscan influence. She was born in 1284. Married to Auzias de Sabran, Count of Arian at 15 (he was 13), they committed themselves to a chaste marriage which ended with Auzias' death in 1323. He was canonized in 1369; a canonization hearing was held for Dauphine in 1363 (see Cambell).

[103] About Jacques de Vitry's role, see Bolton 1978, 253–54; Neel, 240–60.

providing them the support and authority of a recognized cleric. Under the influence of Lutgard of Aywières, Thomas de Cantimpré followed his path and played an equivalent role with Margaret of Ypres and Christina the Astonishing.[104] In spite of their common vision of what such a "hagiobiography" should be and their compliance with the laws of the genre, they cannot erase their own voices and strong personalities.[105] All of the women illustrate the blessing and the curse of being designated by God's grace, and the task of their biographers is to give theological meaning to their abnormal conduct in a way that ordinary folk can understand.[106] Their dedication and mystical experiences are meant to teach the value of lay people's devotion to spiritual life, when it is centred on Christ's incarnation and imitation, and reinforced by the hope of having one's sins redeemed. In this general pattern, the extremes of Christina's behaviour and self-mutilations are legitimized by her mission as intercessor for the souls in Purgatory.[107] In her less theatrical fashion, Margaret of Ypres demonstrates a total indifference to worldly fashions that finds its significance in her renunciation of earthly affection for Christ's love. The same can be said of Lutgard, acting as a successful intercessor against attacks of the demon, or of Marie d'Oignies, who represents the epitome of a mystic woman's life.

---

104 As well as his supplement to de Vitry's biography of Marie.
105 We have adapted the concept of "hagiobiography" – biographies written with the intention of representing life as "more exemplary than real" – from Greenspan's term "autohagiography" (218). See also Heffernan, 5, concerning sacred biography as *imitatio Christi*. These lives are part of the fight against heresy: Lauwers; McNamara 1993 in Wiethaus. For a discussion of the power these women had over their biographers as channels of the divine, see Coakley (1991a), and Coakley (1991b) on how their voices were transcribed and heard. Jacques follows the example of the Fathers who wrote saints lives "in order to strengthen the faith of the weak, instruct the unlearned, incite the sluggish, stir up the devout to imitation, and confuse the rebellious and the unfaithful" (39). Roisin (1947, 79) argues that Vitae could be orally translated for a large illiterate audience. For the Preachers' pastoral care of lay women, see Coakley (1991b).
106 Heffernan, 213; Lauwers, 85–87, relates the production of saintly lives to the expansion of reading.
107 Christina's specialization as intercessor for the souls of the purgatory does not preclude other beguines from playing an important role in that sense (Lauwers 94–98; Newman, 1998). Le Goff's interest in this aspect of their spirituality is limited (318–21 and, about Lutgard, 324–26) and not presented in relation to Dominican preaching, dissociating, for example, Jacques de Vitry's sermons from their lives (298–300). Setting up that context, McNamara (1991, 210–21) situates women's assistance to the dead in Purgatory within their larger commitment to charity. For the preceding period, see McGuire.

Yvette of Huy belonged to the same group. She is presented as example for conversion, living as a recluse after her married life, active in the redemption of sins of a sexual nature.

In contrast to these lives, where each individual account is transcended in order to provide a spiritual lesson to the reader, Douceline's vita conveys the Franciscan message, with the primary objective of promoting her own way of relaying that message through her institution. This author generally remains in the background, avoiding any overt reference to herself. Vitry and Cantimpré, on the other hand, demonstrate their command of the rhetoric of the genre. The topoi of professing their own ineptitude and humility and their authentication of the facts by presenting them as first-hand information or learnt from reliable witnesses, are commonplaces which both biographers carefully develop. Other manifestations of their compliance with the rules of good writing are their introductory procedures, such as explaining the circumstances of the enterprise, the dedication of the work to its sponsor, and the exposition of its main divisions. More revealing are their relatively frequent interventions and comments which exhibit their familiarity with the scriptures or the writings of the Fathers as well as convey their own views.[108] Their theological approach is reflected in the very structure of their works, their divisions reflecting the recognized stages on the path of perfection.[109]

If Philippine briefly sacrifices to the compulsory humility topos and takes pains to provide evidence for the authenticity of Douceline's miracles, she does not indulge any overt display of scriptural knowledge, even if she consents to a few quotations in Latin,[110]

---

[108] For example on women inciting to sexual sin, on greed and other sins, on communion or the gift of prophecy. See Lutgard (Thomas de Cantimpré 1991, 84) for comments on the Song of Songs; Oignies (Jacques de Vitry, 39–40) for examples from Jerome and Gregory the Great; Lutgard (Thomas de Cantimpré 1991, 55) for women leading to pollution; Yvette de Huy about greed (Hugh of Floreffe, 55), on communion (112) and on the gift of prophecy (107).

[109] Goodich, 67: The gifts of the Holy Spirit are enumerated by Jacques de Vitry as the chapter headings of the Life of Marie d'Oignies; Thomas de Cantimpré's Life of Lutgard of Aywières is divided in three parts illustrating the three stages on the path of perfection (see Roisin 1943 about the evolution of his hagiographic style).

[110] It is significant that, although Philippine clearly wants the listener or reader to be aware that she is familiar with Latin, the few phrases she employs are taken either from familiar psalms or from the Holy Office. Moreover, she introduces Latin phrases either as quotations from Douceline or to indicate when the office is being said, see 9:69, 10:12, 16:26 and 13:6, 14:11, 14:22.

nor does she make any clear statement of her own opinions. This does not mean that her work lacks sophistication. Brunel-Lobrichon has discussed the beauty of a text which philologists have considered a most remarkable piece of Occitan literature since Paul Meyer published some pages in 1871.[111]

This vita is as well structured as the lives written by the author's male counterparts, in part because of the influence of Bonaventure's biography of St. Francis, the very text that transported Douceline into rapture when she read the life of the saint.[112] An Occitan version of the *Legenda major* was prepared at about the same date as Philippine's text[113] and the parallels between both lives go beyond their similar division in fifteen chapters. Many details in Douceline's experiences can be directly related to anecdotes recounted about St. Francis. Douceline's own constant references to his saintliness and his dedication to poverty, as well as to his holy stigmata (1:2; 5:9; 9:42; 9:44) are not just the result of her brother Hugh of Digne's teaching, but manifest her personal knowledge and interpretation of the saint's life. She demonstrates her attachment to the virtue of humility in choosing – as Francis himself did – someone in the community whom she could obey (4:9).[114] Other striking correspondences are the role played by birds – she is ravished by their singing (9:19)[115] – and their similar attitude toward the other sex, the sight of whom must be avoided. Both complied with that prohibition to the extent that Francis scarcely knew any woman by sight, and Douceline "hardly knew any man by his face" (6:4).[116]

One of the influential factors in Douceline's decision to start her own community of beguines was an event which presents a close analogy with an incident that occurred once to Francis.[117] On his way to Siena, three poor women appeared to him, who were exactly alike in height, age and appearance and greeted him with a new salutation:

111 Brunel-Lobrichon (1988a, 42) quotes an enthusiast, Ernest Renan, who considers the vita a literary masterpiece.
112 Albanés, 101. Bonaventure's *Legenda major* was made Francis's official biography in 1266. According to Durieux, its Occitan translation was made at the end of the thirteenth century by friends of Peter-John Olivi (89).
113 Brunel-Lobrichon 1988a, mentions the edition by Ingrid Arthur (47).
114 Habig, 673.
115 Habig, 695 sq.
116 Habig, 666.
117 Habig, 683.

"Welcome, Lady Poverty".[118] It was also on the road, on her way from the hospital in Hyères with three companions, that Douceline met two women and a little girl wearing black clothing, their faces covered with veils of white cloth (2:4). She saw in this encounter the sign that she should not only found a community but also adopt the black habit the ladies of her vision wore, with the mantle covering the head in imitation of God's holy mother.[119] It therefore seems clear and entirely appropriate that, while Douceline modelled the structure and regulation of her community, as well as her own conduct, on the life of St. Francis, Philippine referred to his vita as a model for her own Life of St. Douceline.

Editorial Note

While Douceline was never officially canonized, our text identifies her throughout as "the Blessed Saint Douceline". Indeed, a vital portion of the narrative is concerned with establishing her sanctity, and even shows doubters being convinced by the posthumous appearance of Douceline herself. Thus we have adopted the designation "Saint" employed by the author of our vita.

[118] From the *Vita secunda* by Thomas of Celano, chapter 93, according to Brunel-Lobrichon 1997, 178.
[119] According to the Protoevangelium of James, influential in propagating veneration of Mary (Heffernan, 232). Sisto (44) who mentions the legend, suggests that Douceline might have seen Jewish women in Hyères wearing the blue headband prescribed by Frederick II.

The Life of Saint Douceline, Mother of the Ladies of Roubaud

In the Name of our Lord, here begins the Life of the Blessed Saint Douceline, Mother of the Ladies of Roubaud

Chapter One

Chapter one tells of the way she lived in secular dress and of her upbringing in relation to her parents.

1. There was a man of the city of Digne, a great and wealthy merchant called Bérenguier; he had as his wife a virtuous woman named Hugue, who was from Barjols; and both of them were good and righteous in following the law of Our Lord. They lived a just and holy life, according to their position, loyally keeping and observing God's commandments. With great piety and generosity they welcomed the poor and served the sick and the suffering in their home, and they gave generously to them from their possessions, with great compassion, spending what God gave to them in holy works of piety.

2. According to the word of Jesus Christ, who is a testimony of truth, from a good root comes a good tree, all of whose fruits are good; in the same way, since the parents were virtuous, the children who were born of these good parents through the great generosity of God's kindness, were good, just and holy. Living a saintly life, they gave to Our Lord, through their holiness, two great lights that shone night and day, namely Brother Hugh of Digne, of venerable memory, who was a Friar Minor and most ardent preacher of the truth of Jesus Christ, in the order of Saint Francis. His preaching gave light and warmth like the sun, for it wondrously led men to serve God and to leave the world.[1] Both of them, by the brilliance of their life and their perfection, shone in the eyes of sinners and of the just; they were the splendour of all holiness, and, by their examples of virtue, they shone and they lit up the estate of holy penitence.

3. The second light, no less luminous in the holiness of her life, was my lady Saint Douceline of Digne, who was very gentle and worthy,[2] for God visited blessings of gentleness upon her. In her early childhood, before she knew her prayers or letters, when they were living in the town of Barjols, she would go out, through God's urging, onto the

---

[1] There are comments on the charisma of Hugh's preaching in Salimbene (217, 226) and in Joinville's *Vie de Saint Louis*, when he preached before the king in 1248.

[2] It is impossible to reproduce in the translation the play on the two words composing Douceline's name: she is *douce* (=sweet) and *digne* (=worthy).

terraces of her father's house, kneel with bare knees on the small stones she found on the ground, join her hands in prayer to God and turn her face to heaven, not knowing how to say anything. This was a demonstration that God was working a great exercise of prayer in her to which she had to give herself, and it showed the grace of the marvelous contemplation that she had to make to heaven; before she knew how to talk properly, she made the sign of prayer and of contemplation, showing, in this way, with what uprightness and purity her heart had to be given entirely to God.

4. The more she grew in intellect, the more she gave herself to praying to God and to prayer; and when someone would go looking for her, expecting to find her playing with the other children, she would be found hiding in order to pray to God in the most secret places of the house. She willingly sought out solitary places where she could pray and she hid as much as she could so that she might not be seen in her praying. Each day this maiden became better and better, and as she grew older she grew also in virtues and in good habits. She strictly obeyed her father and her mother, and willingly did what they commanded. When the mother died, they moved to Hyères, where they lived from that time on.

5. Her father wanted her to serve the poor whom, for the love of God, he was accustomed to looking after in his home. The good man brought home the sick and the suffering that he found in the streets and by the roads, and said: "My daughter, I am bringing and giving profit to you." She received them joyfully and with great humility, obeying her father's orders; and she cared for them with great devotion, and was not afraid to submit her body to whatever was needed for them. Many times, for the love of the Lord, she washed their feet, picked the vermin from their legs and their heads, and cared for their wounds. The more horrible and frightful they were because of their diseases and wounds, the more zealous she was to serve them, and the more care she gave them; full of charity, she would carry them when they were not able to walk.

6. One time, a poor man came to her who was suffering greatly and was very sick, and he was so weak that he had her carry him. She served him with great kindness, as was her custom. And the sick man asked her, out of his great necessity, to put her hand on his chest. When she heard this, she was alarmed because of her great modesty and her great sense of propriety, and she began to consider whether she would do it, because he was a man. Understanding the shame from her great modesty, he said to her, "My daughter, do not be ashamed on my account, for I myself would not be ashamed to make you known to my father." And as soon as he said this, the poor man suddenly disappeared and she saw him no more.

7. Another time, it happened that, while she was caring for a sick man who was dying, she fell asleep from extreme exhaustion. And the poor man whom she was looking after was shown to her in very great glory, and with indescribable splendour. And she saw a beautiful garden in which he was enjoying himself in a wonderful meadow, and she saw him amid the greatest delights. As soon as she awoke, she went to look at him and found him dead. Throughout the time that she remained in that state, the Lord gave her many other consolations, which showed her the great pleasure that he took in the services that she rendered in his name to the unfortunate sick.

8. She attended to this service of charity as long as her father lived; and she did not abandon it afterwards, but continued her holy works of piety all the time that she was in secular clothing. She divided the night into three parts: she would spend the greatest part in reading and in prayer; next she would rest; then she would get up and say her matins. Afterwards, she would never return to her bed, but she would spend the time in works of piety or in prayer. When she could not pray during the day because of her work, then the following night, instead of resting, she would make up for what she had not been able to do. She spent her days in serving the sick or in works of piety, and her nights in prayer.

9. Her modesty was so great that she would not set her eyes on a man; on her face, which was very beautiful, one could see reserve, propriety and modesty; and above all, she avoided all friendship with men, and all their conversation.

10. Soon after, she began to mortify her flesh and applied herself to it so courageously that she spared her body nothing. Secretly, so that no one would know about it, she wore a hair shirt made of pigskin, which was rough and hard and dug into her flesh to the point that often she could not remove it; and when she did take it off, her body was left torn and covered with cuts from it. Once it happened that it had so embedded itself in her body that no matter what she did she could not remove it. Then, compelled by necessity, she called her servant, who was a woman she trusted, and this woman removed it

from her by force, tearing off her skin with the pigskin. And immediately she made her swear to say nothing about the matter.

11.   She would bind her body tightly with a knotted cord, and at the place where the knots dug into her flesh there were often worms. In addition to all of this, she continually wore a girdle of iron, without anyone knowing it, in order to further afflict her body; and over it she would wear beautiful, elegant robes, as if she loved colourful fabrics. And when it happened that her servant found out anything about the harshness of her penitence, as soon as she was aware of it, she made her swear to say nothing about it.

12.   For penitence she would sleep on a little bit of straw in the corner of her room; and so that sleep would bring her no rest, she would attach a rope above her bed, and she would tie the other end of the rope around herself so that as soon as she moved, the rope would pull on her and she would wake up; and she would get up immediately to say her matins with reverence and she would begin to read.

13.   In this way she forcefully subdued her own body with hair shirts, just as Saint Cecilia, the blessed virgin, did; and she spent her nights, just as that same virgin did, in prayer and in holy vigils.[3] This is how she lived while she was in secular dress.

Chapter Two

Chapter two tells of how she put on the habit of penitence.

1.   After the death of her father, she devoted herself to her works of piety more than ever, and, in the ardour of her charity, gave herself entirely to the service of the poor. She visited the poor who were sick, wherever she knew of them, for the love of the Lord, and with great compassion; she gave them abundant alms and all possible service. She was entirely consumed by the fire of charity, wanting to do more and to find ways of serving God better. For she had no love

---

3   According to Jacobus de Voragine's *Golden Legend*, St. Cecilia prayed night and day that God help her to protect her virginity. When she was married to Valerian, she wore a hair shirt and succeeded in convincing him to remain chaste and have a spiritual marriage. *The Golden Legend of Jacobus de Voragine. Translated and adapted from the Latin by Granger Ryan and Helmut Ripperger* (New York: Arno Press, 1969), 689–695.

for the world, and despised it as nothing, wanting to leave behind everything earthly.

2. At that time, there was no house of beguines, and no one had heard of them in Provence. And a marvelous thing happened to her at the town of Hyères. It was her custom to visit the hospitals often, to serve the sick with great love, and to do her best to comfort them. Moved by her example, many other women would accompany her to do these works for the love of the Lord.

3. One day she was returning with three others from a hospital in Hyères, a short distance from the castle and, as she had been wanting to do for a long time, she asked Our Lord with all her heart to let her find an order and a way of life that would be pleasing to God, and that might put her into the state that would be the most pleasing to him; and as they were returning from visiting the poor and accomplishing the holy task of looking after the sick, the visitation of God came upon them to comfort the Saint; and it happened in the following way.

4. Suddenly two humble ladies who looked alike and who were walking along with great modesty, their faces discreetly covered with veils of white cloth, appeared to them on the road; and all their clothing was black.[4] They led a small girl who was walking with them; and greeted them most joyously. Stopping in front of Douceline, they looked at her. When the holy woman saw them, she was at once filled with great elation; completely filled with ardour she asked them who they were and from what order. Then all three together placed on their heads the mantles they were carrying, saying: "We are from that order which is pleasing to God." And pointing to the veils that they were wearing, they said: "Put this on and follow us." And at once they disappeared, and no one could tell what had become of them.

5. They immediately ran after the ladies, but they could not find them anywhere. They questioned the people who were coming and going in the street where those women who had spoken to them had gone, describing the habit they were wearing and everything about

---

4   On his way to Siena, Francis had met three women who looked alike and they
greeted him with the salutation of: "Welcome, Lady Poverty" (Habig 683).

their appearance, to find out if anyone had encountered them. Everyone answered that they had seen no ladies but them. And although the place where they had appeared was a large open space, they were never able to see them again.

6. The habit worn by those ladies and their modest manner had never been seen before. And they all remained full of joy and great amazement. But the Saint, through the spirit of God, immediately understood the meaning of the invitation that they had issued to follow them, and she firmly resolved in her heart to take up that way of life and to follow that example rather than any other.

7. At that time, the holy man who was her brother, Friar Hugh of Digne, had gone to Paris, and had arranged for her to be accepted by the Franciscan Sisters of Genoa, although she had been accepted by many other religious houses in Provence. When he returned, she spoke with him and revealed to him what had happened to her, speaking with the greater confidence we believe she had received in the meantime. For the holiness of the work that she did in starting her establishment, the type of habit that she took, the high degree of her perfection, and the saving of that holy foundation, showed and convinced people that she was assured of God's goodness and that he wanted her to take on that appearance and that way of life.

8. When the holy brother Hugh had carefully listened to her and knew her intention, he did not want her to enter any other order; rather, instead of any other, he wanted her to take up that form and way of living, based on the life that she led. And so she took up that life for herself and for her establishment and followed it from that time on. Then, with great disregard for the world, she immediately gave up the clothes she was wearing, and with great ardour she dressed herself in black, in the colour and style of the habit of the ladies that she had seen. With a wonderful joyousness of spirit, she put on the same kind of headband that they were wearing and took the veil with great devotion and with great joy in her soul.

9. Then, filled with fervour and with love for Our Lord, she placed the mantle on her head, as a sign of the passion of Jesus Christ; and from then on she always wore the mantle on her head, in reverence and following the example of the mother of God who, she said, always covered her head with the mantle after the passion of her son. We believe that she learned this through a revelation from Our Lord, for she related with certainty that as long as the Virgin remained in this world, after the death of her son, she wore the sign of his death and the reminder of his passion. And, as much as possible, the holy woman modeled herself on her and ordered her whole life according to that of Our Lady, and she conducted herself following her example, with the advice of her brother.

10. And thus kindled and burning with the fire of the charity of Jesus Christ, in great ardour of love, she gave herself entirely to God, with no turning back; and with all her heart she dedicated her virginity to Our Lord during a sermon given by the Saint at Hyères, and she made her vow with great fervour before all the people, placing her hands in those of her brother. Many other women followed her example, so that there were 131 who pledged their virginity to Our Lord; and many others still, more than 80, who made a promise of chastity, following her example at the time of the sermon, and they placed their hands in the hands of the holy father.

11. The holy mother wanted to be called a beguine, through the love of Our Lady, who was her model; for she said that Our Lady was the first beguine, which we believe she learned through the inspiration of Our Lord God. And so that she might resemble her more closely, she made a vow of poverty; for the mother of God was poor in this world, and for the love of her she wanted to be called poor and to live in poverty. The holy mother was the first beguine in Provence and she was the origin of all those who took that name. And she trained them for the service of God. But there were some who wanted to be exactly like her.

Chapter Three

Chapter three tells of the manner in which she organized her institution and her order.

1. At the time that the holy father, Friar Hugh of Digne, began preaching at Hyères, many people were drawn to God through his preaching, and were anxious to leave the world and with great love take up the way of penitence and virtue. Of those, the holy mother wanted the first to be her two nieces whose father had died. She drew them to God, took them to be with her, and made them beguines.

2.   Later, when the renown of her holiness and virtue had spread, at the time when the Saint was preaching fervently, many pious ladies were greatly moved by his words and came to join with her through great devotion, and took up her way of life and her fine doctrine. And they made a home for themselves that they called Roubaud, outside the city, because they said that living among people would present them with too many impediments to doing good. And the holy mother wanted them to remove themselves from the world as far as possible and avoid it so that they might offer their whole heart to God more fully and more freely.

3.   But the devotion of the people increased when they saw her example; and, moved also by the marvelous sermons of the Saint who was drawing them to God, and on fire for Our Lord, many others, by the will of God, virgins and widows, and even married women, leaving their husbands and children, came to her and placed themselves very humbly and with great devotion and reverence, in her company.

4.   When the holy mother saw that her humble company was growing little by little, through God's grace, she wanted to write a rule and way of living for herself and for her daughters. To do this more faithfully and more correctly, she wanted to have the advice of the holy father in the writing of it. And so she went to him with her humble company, humbly and devotedly asking him to give them a form and manner of living for God. And he gave it to them – a true one – so that whoever was willing to follow it would have no doubt of receiving salvation.

5.   After she had begun her institution in Hyères and had founded a convent there, she thought at once of doing more good works, and she took one of the most perfect of her ladies, and went away with her to Marseilles, and there she established another house of Roubaud to the glory of God. In that place, many good people brought her their daughters and their female relatives and offered them to her in great piety. Soon, through God's grace, they were great in number.

6.   And every day God multiplied and increased this holy institution in the two convents. For this the holy mother gave thanks to Our Lord God with all her heart. And she made every effort to see that none of them sinned, not only in deeds, but also in words, and she wanted them to guard against setting a bad example. And she taught them to attend to holy prayer and to be faithful: "For", she said, "that is where the security of his establishment is to be found and the means of growing in all virtues."

7. And she taught them how to pray, and to feel and weep for the passion of Christ. "For all Christians", she said, "have a great duty to remember the passion of the Lord, at least once a day. For we must never forget this blessing, but continually carry in our hearts the death of Christ, for which we live as widows, with our heads covered."

8. And the Saint said that a beguine was made for weeping, and not for singing: "For", she said, "she must continually carry Jesus Christ crucified in her heart, just as she wears the sign of the pain of his death on her covered head, and shows it on her face."

9. And these good women learned the holy lessons that she taught them willingly and with great love. They lived in great fear of Our Lord, and in obedience to the holy mother. Their conversation was completely angelic, for they lived the life of angels among the people, to the point that their great purity in words and actions seemed not to be that of women; it seemed to be angels teaching such piety.

10. Many times the holy father Hugh told them, when he was exhorting them to grow in the holy virtues: "Truly," the holy man would say, "if you persevere like this, you will wing your way to God." They lived in great charity for each other, and they all loved one another in God. Keeping and fulfilling his holy commandments, they exerted themselves in all good works of piety and charity. They spent all their time in this way, and they spread forth the fragrance of a good reputation among the people, through their great virtue and their fine example.

Chapter Four

Chapter four tells of her humility and her obedience.

1. In all these things, the holy mother was their guide and mistress, and she delighted in Our Lord. She took great joy in seeing their holy way of life and the growth of her institution; and, by her manner, she was an example of complete perfection among them. For she was humble of heart, having such a great and perfect humility that, in her eyes, she was vile and as nothing before God. For that reason she appeared poor and despised to people in the world, and she wanted to be scorned by everyone.

2.   She would often tell the others, when she was admonishing them, that what she prized the most in her institution was great humility and the scorn of people. And whenever someone said to her, "Mother, everyone scorns us and people hold our estate in great disdain", she would answer most perfectly: "Truly, it is my honour and my glory, my joy and my crown that the world holds us in great scorn, and that everyone disdains us." And she would say that the name beguine pleased her greatly and that she held it in great esteem because it was humble and scorned by the world's pride.

3.   She had a great horror of honour and praise when they were given to her, and it distressed her greatly to receive them. Whenever people would kneel before her in great devotion and reverence upon seeing her, she would show extreme displeasure; especially when the great lords, kings and princes, counts and barons would come in great devotion to visit her and to pay reverence to her, when the renown of her great holiness had spread far and wide. She would be greatly distressed by the honour that she had received and would remain grieved by it. For a long time, and especially on that day, she would remain greatly ashamed among the others; it seemed that a great misfortune had befallen her. And she would say to our Lord, with much bitterness in her heart, "Lord, here I am, poor and vile, yet esteemed in people's eyes. This should not be. I pray you, Lord, with all my heart, to confound me in the opinion of everyone."

4.   She could not bear that anyone would kneel to her, even a child; before they could bend down, she herself would kneel. She strove above all to establish her order on humility. She told all her daughters to keep this virtue as the foundation of her entire institution. For that reason, she did not want to allow them to have a church built, or to have any other worldly things of value; she did not want them to acquire skill in letters or to sing the office, or to have anything that would raise them too high.

5.   She would often say to them when she was exhorting them to great virtue, "Remain, my daughters, remain in the humility in which you were called to Our Lord God, and do not try to rise higher; for it is certain that if you live in sincerity, God will glorify you, and will make people understand that you are sincere women. As soon as you change, God will make people feel the opposite; in that case he would make the stones speak and they would say that you are not what you should be. Keep to the way of humility in all things and strive to keep it in your heart, like a precious treasure. For you well know that humility is the particular way of salvation, the nourishment of all purity, and the root of perfection; without it nothing can be pleasing to God. Therefore, make every effort to possess it. We have the perfect example of it in Our Lady who leads us in everything."

6. This virtue of true humility made her very pleasing and familiar to God and worthy of every respect from the people. So great was the dignity people sensed in her, because of this virtue, that when even the great barons, the powerful lords, princes, kings and counts came in great devotion to see her, they could not keep themselves from bending their knees in the greatest respect. This was very distressing to the humble virgin. When these people had visited her and spoken with her, they would depart marveling and would go away greatly edified.

7. Once it happened that a great man from Lombardy came to visit her, and when he had spoken with her, he earnestly begged her to reveal to him, after having obtained knowledge of it from Our Lord, one thing that he greatly desired to know. And the Saint humbly answered him that she was not worthy of knowing the secrets of God, and that she would not be able to make that prayer; that she was a sinner and should not engage in spiritual matters.

8. This increased the man's devotion, and he said that he believed that she could certainly reveal it to him, and if she was willing to do so, he promised that he would provide enough funds that her establishment would always be maintained. But God's Saint would have nothing to do with his promises, for she did not act out of pretence or hypocrisy. So she excused herself all the more from doing it and answered him humbly. Then the man departed from her, very disconsolate, for no matter what he did, he was not able to learn what he wanted so much to know.

9.   Her humility was not feigned, but true; and this virtue was like a mother within her, nourishing her and making her grow continually in God. So that she might increase in this virtue in more ways she, who was the general prioress of both convents, wanted to have a sister to be her prioress, whom she would humbly obey and she promised obedience to her with great devotion. In order to be always obedient through the love of the Lord, she also swore obedience to Brother Jaucelin, a holy man, who was a minister of the Friars Minor in Provence, and who was later the bishop of Orange; as long as she lived, she was humbly obedient to him.

10.   At that time, King Charles I, brother of the good king Saint Louis of France, was count of Provence; and so many evil things were told to him about the Friars Minor that his anger toward the order was so great that none of the brothers dared to come before him. It happened that the countess had a dream that came about in this way. She was great with child and she was so heavy that she herself and all those who saw her, even the doctors, despaired for her life and for that of the child. Everyone was very afraid that the child might perish before it could be baptized.   .

11.   One night, in a dream, the countess saw a fine lady wearing the modest habit of a beguine, who came very humbly to see her, accompanied by two others, and who spoke to her with great kindness. And after the holy lady had prayed, she was certainly saved from the peril of her delivery, and she escaped from any danger, both she and her child. And this same dream came to her on three nights. And the third time, she revealed this to the count, explaining her perilous position to him, for she was very frightened. She told him that without the help of great prayers she did not believe she could escape death. And she added that she was sure God had not shown her this dream for no reason.

12.   Then the count asked if in all his territories anyone knew such a woman that God might want to send to help her. And by the will of God, he learned of the holy lady. When the count learnt that she was Hugh of Digne's sister and heard of her virtues and humility, he had great faith in her and sent for her. As soon as the countess saw her, she said that she was truly the one that she had seen in her dream, and that she firmly believed, without any doubt, that through her prayers she would escape from her peril. And she did not let her go away from her.

13. The dream that she had came true, just as she had previously told it to the count. With the Saint in fervent prayer, the lady, by the grace of God, bore a daughter. Therefore the count and the countess wanted her to be her godmother and to baptize her, and with great respect they made her their commother.[5] The mother was convinced that it was through her that God had saved her from the peril of death, just as the dream had shown her. And the count believed this, as did all his court.

14. Because of the fine example that they saw in her, and because of her humility, the count had such devotion that, for love of her, he restored the Friars and the whole order to his good graces; they had all considered themselves dead and had been living in great fear. And by her humility, she restored them all into the king's graces. And so, the count's anger, which neither the power nor the wisdom of men nor of the Friars had been able to temper, the simplicity of the humble Douceline was able to assuage.

Chapter Five

Chapter five deals with the vow of holy poverty and of the manner in which she kept it with extreme love and diligence and of the great disdain she had for temporal things.

1. To acquire the kingdom of heaven, there is no treasure as deserving as poverty. Jesus Christ alone taught this and gave it to his disciples, that is to say to the holy apostles, as their principal foundation; for Poverty of spirit alone is the price of the kingdom of heaven, and to buy it she sells everything she has, and gives it to the poor. For this reason, the holy mother, my lady Douceline, had contempt for the whole world, out of her desire for the heavenly realm. In order to acquire and possess it, she abandoned everything, and gave away her riches and treasures in exchange for poverty, for it is only in this way that one can acquire it.

2. She was the good merchant woman who, wanting to buy the precious jewel of the Gospel of Christ that she had found – holy

---

5 According to the *Oxford English Dictionary*, the name commother is used for the "relationship to the other god-parents and the actual parents of the child".

poverty – gave up all her earthly possessions for it. And truly, it was the precious treasure of the Gospel, hidden in the field; and to obtain it she generously distributed everything she had and gave it all to the poor, for the love of Christ who was crucified, poor and suffering, and for the love of his mother, who was queen of the world, because she wanted to be poor and suffering in this world as the Lord was.

3. For love of them, this holy virgin, although her friends loved her very much and cherished her, renounced all the treasures and riches of her father, and of her other friends with great contempt, and fervently embraced poverty out of a sense of humility. She made a vow in the hands of the holy father, Brother Hugh of Digne, to keep the holy poverty of Jesus Christ with great ardour, just as Saint Francis observed it and passed it on. That is to say, she had nothing of her own, not even a robe or vestment; she had no coat or outer garment or undergarment. Rather, when she needed to change her clothes, her ladies had to provide them for the love of the Lord; apart from that, she accepted nothing that was given to her.

4. Even the sheets on the bed in which she lay in her final illness were not hers; and they had to lend her a robe. When her soul had left her body, they could find nothing with which they could cover her; so one of her daughters took off her own robe so that they could put it on her. Even the veil and the headband were lent to her – in short, all her clothing – for this holy poor friend of Our Lord had shown faithfulness and wanted to be faithful to Lady Poverty to the end, firmly keeping the vow that she had made.

5. She did not want to take or keep alms that were too valuable; and if at any time they were offered to her she would have them held in common, or she would give them to the Friars, or divide them among poor people. She would not accept alms that were a form of tax from anyone, for any reason, for she said that it would go against the vow of the Gospel.

6. It happened one time that a noble lady of Provence by the name of Lady Philippine of Porcellet, Lady of Artignols, came to the holy mother with great devotion, and entered Roubaud to be her daughter. And once she was there, she saw the holy mother living in poverty and receiving the meagre alms that were given to her. And she saw her so destitute that, when she was ill, she often did not have a penny to make herself better. And so this lady, who was a very rich woman, had compassion for her. And one day she went to her in secret and, kneeling humbly, begged her to accept her help, saying that she was ready and willing to look after her needs and give her the necessities of life for as long as she lived.

7. After thanking her, the holy mother kindly and humbly answered her: "May God neither want nor permit me ever to do anything against the vow of holy poverty, Lady Philippine. You can be sure, my lady, that I will not take anything from anyone of whatever dignity, to assure my life; for it does not seem to me that I would be keeping the law of poverty faithfully if anyone were looking after my needs." She never wanted to take what was offered to her, but she said that she would sometimes accept the alms that were given to her for the love of God, when she needed them.

8. When the count of Provence, who was later the king of Sicily, had seen her and recognized her holiness, he was greatly devoted to her; and each year he would send her ten pounds in alms. The holy one of God did not want to accept these alms or keep them for herself; instead, she would put the ten pounds into the common purse. The Sisters provided for her from that as they saw fit, without her asking them for anything. And she took as pure alms what was given to her.

9. In this way, the Saint strictly wanted to keep and maintain the vow of holy poverty. She wanted to spend her whole life in suffering and great privation as an example and for the love of the poor mother of Jesus Christ, in whose clothing she had dressed herself. Just as Saint Francis had adopted the clothing of the Lord, she took those of the mother. And because humility preserves poverty and poverty nourishes humility, she joined them together, like two sisters of the mother of God, for these virtues were very familiar to her, and shone greatly both in the son and in the mother.

10. Because she desired to have both of these virtues, and loved them very much, she wanted to possess them both at the same time, as foundations. For she was the house of Our Lord, in which the spirit of God resided. And this Lord, for the love of whom she lived in want, mercifully and kindly looked after all her needs. Her poverty was richer than the abundance of those who love the world's wealth. For, as often in those situations where money is insufficient, her poverty was great abundance, as is said of Saint Francis.

11.   When the Sisters saw that their mother had fully embraced the holy poverty of the Gospel, they followed in her footsteps and wanted to make the vow. But the holy father, Brother Hugh, would not allow it and advised them against it, preferring them to live modestly and to be able to give alms, for that is not a safe thing for women, especially for young women. And so the holy mother, on the holy father's advice, asked them to choose moderate poverty, so that they might be able to provide for their needs in a limited and modest way, and so that they might faithfully serve the Lord with their own money and guard against excess. Lovingly they accepted this decision, with a great desire to follow and keep it always.

12.   Because the holy mother knew that there is no benefit in riches, but that they are often the occasion of great suffering, she did not think of obtaining any other possessions for them; for the mother did not want their hearts to be attached to anything in this world, but only to what they needed in order to live. Once a very rich man said that he would like to support her house. He wanted to give great sums to enrich it, and he wanted to do wonderful things. But the holy mother would never consent to it and would not accept it, for she wanted her daughters to live modestly and to serve God with their meagre resources, supporting the poor among them, and caring for one another. And they have kept and observed this wish right up to this day.

Chapter Six

Chapter six tells of the austerity of her life, and of the great exercise of good works to be found in her and in the others.

1.   Because the holy mother was the head and mistress of all the others, she had to be an example to them in all virtues. Not only was she the leader and director of those in Roubaud who were under her allegiance, and of whom she was the mother, but she was also the leader and mistress of those who, by her example, became beguines on the street near Roubaud, in Marseilles and also in Hyères. For in each place, whenever she was there, she governed them and corrected them when it was needed. All of them, when they were beginning, made a vow and promised obedience to her.

2. That is why, when she saw that by her example so many were encouraged to serve Jesus Christ, she herself was encouraged even more. Moreover, she restrained the desires of all her feelings with such strict discipline that she barely ate what was necessary to sustain her natural life. Her moderation in eating and drinking was so great that she provided an example of edification, not only when she abstained, but even when she ate.

3. In all things her observance was strict and severe, and she kept a scrupulous abstinence, condemning every pleasure in herself. She was careful to maintain purity of body and soul, in herself and in the others. That is why she not only taught that the body should be mortified, but she also wished that the external senses be watched with extreme care.

4. She ordered the shunning of the company of men, their words and their looks, and required this, without any mercy, not only of her own women but of all those who wanted to live under her direction. She herself hardly knew any man by his face. And so, if she saw any one of her women of Roubaud raise her head to look at or listen to one, even a close relative, she would reprimand her very sharply and punish her severely. For, she would say, she did not want any of them to take pleasure in any other but Our Lord Jesus Christ.

5. One time, one of the young ones at Roubaud, who was not more that seven years old, had looked at some men who were working there. When the holy mother learned of it, she beat her harshly, to the point that blood ran from her sides; and she told her that she would make a sacrifice of her to God. To the end of her days, the girl thanked her for that, for she attested that this beating served to put her soul right with Our Lord.

6. She would sharply correct any woman who had given herself to God if she even spoke to a man. She said that it was not a safe thing to do. "I am sure", she would say, "that you will not speak with them for long about Our Lord before you will become colder, less good and less devoted in the end than your were in the beginning." She was displeased when she saw it, outside of confession. This counsel was closely followed by her daughters even with their close relatives, unless there was a very good reason, and then they spoke as little as possible. Not only did she not allow them to speak with men; they were most strongly to avoid talking about them; and if she found that any had done this, she used to punish them very severely, to their great shame.

7.   She did not want her daughters to look for consolation, whether great or small, except in Jesus Christ, for whom she was faithfully raising them. She wanted them to feed continually on his words, she said, so that, in speaking of him, they would all be burning with his love. Therefore, none of them would have dared to talk with another about her relatives, and even less about others, so that no other love but that of Jesus Christ would enter their heart. She wanted her daughters to faithfully observe these things and she commanded them to avoid the opposite with great vigilance.

8.   The holy mother did not want them to be idle or to wander, either in their hearts or in their words; rather she wanted them to practise every good work. And so she exhausted them in serving the sick. She wanted them to do these acts of service not just for the Friars, but for the poor who were sick, even in hospitals. So that she might be an example to the others, she was the first to do all these things. She wanted these holy works to be done unceasingly, and she would not tolerate anyone allowing her body too much rest.

9.   She made them all avoid excessive talking. "For", she would say, "one cannot let oneself talk a great deal without sinning and without coming gradually to words that displease God." They were especially to avoid, more than death, talking among themselves about the world's vanities or about anything that pertained to the world; and if she found out that anyone had sinned in this way through her foolishness, she would punish her terribly. For she would not suffer anything that could sully the pure soul offered to God that was in her care.

10.   She strenuously avoided lies, declaring that anyone who lies cannot please God. This was her great concern in chapter, where she said that if she found someone lying, she would sacrifice her with her own hands. She wanted them to make every effort to closely guard and rule their tongues and she would not allow them to give themselves to idle words; "Because these can lead to other words", she would say. The holy mother also said, "Just as the wind carries away the dew of heaven and prevents it from falling and watering the grasses, in the same way pointless talking and idleness prevent God's grace from entering the soul and watering it."

11. She avoided these things and corrected them rigorously in chapters and in her visits; for, in order to live more purely for God, she was in the habit of visiting each convent from time to time. And although she was very kind and humble, and wonderfully caring, she was fearsome in her reprimands and punishments, and acted with great authority. At chapter or in her visits, when she was meting out punishment, there was no one who did not tremble upon seeing her authority, and it seemed that her authority represented the judgement of God. Although she maintained harsh justice in her punishments, when she could see humble repentance, she was wondrously moved to forgive always fairly, provided that the gentle pardon was not the occasion for another failing

12. She tempered all of this with great kindness, so that her punishments left marvelous consolation. Her corrections, even when they were harsh, were always consoling. While her example led the others to austerity and while she urged them to live with great discipline in all things, she did not like the rigour of austerity without discretion. Singularity especially displeased her. She avoided it and would not allow it in any of them. Rather, for safety, she wanted them to keep to a middle way and to follow it as much as each one was able.

13. She continually washed herself, day and night, in a great shower of tears so that her soul would always be pleasing to God. She did not excuse her body or its weakness, so that even when she was ill, she did not let that hour of the night pass in which she made it a custom to weep.

14. Many times, the ladies who were caring for her in her illness had proof of this. They would think she was sleeping, but when the hour of midnight came, she was so accustomed to the practice that she would not be able to sleep or rest. She would spend all that time, until after matins, in a great abundance of tears. Although she hid this as much as she could and wiped away the signs of it so that it would not be known, it was impossible for the others not to hear it, when her weeping was so great. Especially at those times when they stayed near her because of her great suffering, she was unable to keep them from knowing about it.

15. As a result of her continual tears, she would have terrible headaches, so that she was often unable to eat for a day and a night, and could not open her eyes. She would barely be able to talk and could not hear a word. With all that, she did not cease her weeping at the appointed hours to which she was accustomed. No matter what illness she might have, she did not fail in her devotion in any way.

Chapter Seven

Chapter seven is about her goodness and her innocence

1.   So great was the Saint's natural goodness of heart that she could not allow animals or birds to be killed, if she knew of it; she was moved by a feeling of great compassion, especially for those creatures that symbolically represent Christ, according to the Scriptures.

2.   Whenever anyone brought live birds to her for her pleasure, she would not let them be killed; rather, after she had enjoyed them for a little while, speaking of Our Lord who had created them, her spirit would be lifted to God, and she would let them go, saying: "Praise the Lord, your creator." Seeing lambs or sheep would bring her great delight and would make her feel a wonderful love for the true lamb, Jesus Christ, because it made her remember him.

3.   This virtue led her to experience all the suffering that she saw or heard of. In particular, when she felt that souls which had been redeemed by the blood of Christ were stained with sin, she would weep for them tenderly, like a mother, as if they were her children in Christ. And she wanted the others to feel great sorrow and to ask God's mercy for the conversion and salvation of those souls. Even those things that took place far away, the zeal of her love made seem close at hand.

4.   At that time, the Saracens captured the nuns of Antioch; and when she learned of it, this true lover of all purity was very distressed and showed great sorrow.[6] She assembled the chapter and, weeping bitterly, told them all to practise discipline, to fast, to weep and to cry to God with bitter tears for mercy. And she gave the same orders in the other convent at Hyères. Then she said, "We should not be removed from such misfortunes even when they occur overseas; for truly, to the one who does not feel the stranger's adversities, God will

---

6   The city of Antioch was lost to the Saracens in 1260.

bring them upon her head. Each one of us should think that it is because of her own sins that God has abandoned those women."

5. And then she said to Our Lord, with great bitterness of heart, "Lord, why have you permitted this? I am sure that those women have always lived better than I. But my sin has brought harm to them, and it is because of my sins, Lord, that you have forsaken them." And she prostrated herself on the ground with her arms outstretched, in such profound grief that it seemed as if she was about to die. She did not eat or drink all that day. Seeing her in such great sorrow, all the others could do nothing but weep. They were all in great distress.

6. They never dared to tell her about things that had happened which were an offence to God, because they were amazed at how she would be affected by it. She keenly felt God's displeasure and the offence that was given him. Then it would seem as if her heart was broken by the sorrow, because of the compassion that she had for those souls. If it happened that she heard something about it at table, she would be unable to eat.

7. She suffered with all those in affliction, whatever the nature of their misfortune, and she related everything to Christ through the compassion of her love. Once, she heard a woman weeping and crying bitterly because she had lost her husband. When she heard it, the Saint cried out with tears, "Ah! how wretched I am! I have lost my Saviour through sin, and yet I do not lament or weep or grieve for his loss the way this woman does, weeping in great sorrow, for a mortal man." And then the Saint began to cry bitterly, with such great grief and emotion that the hearts of all those who were there were filled with contrition.

8. This virtue of goodness of heart grew so powerfully in her from her childhood, with such a wonderful openness and generosity of heart, that it seemed as if she gave away her heart in compassion when she saw the needs of the poor. So no one dared to tell her of things that would inspire pity, because she would suffer so greatly from it.

Chapter Eight

Chapter eight deals with her fervent charity and with her service to the sick.

1.   Who could describe the fervent love that the true friend of God, my holy lady Douceline, possessed? She was so solidly rooted in the love of God that when she heard anything said about it, she would immediately be stirred and afire, so much so, that in her body and on her face, she showed outward signs of that flame that burned in her heart for the love of the Lord. She seemed all ablaze with that great affection.

2.   To her, this whole world was like a representation of God; everything she saw represented her Lord to her, and by her love she found God in all things. In beautiful things she contemplated the supreme beauty, in melodies God's gentle ways, and she delighted in all the works of Our Lord. There was never a more ardent devotion than this Saint's. The superior love that she had for God joined her so closely to every creature that she recognized that each one of them had a creator and a beginning.

3.   She extended her charity especially to the poor and suffering, whom she served with a marvelous affection, helping all those that she could. And to those she could not supply with temporal things, she willingly gave her whole heart, and subjected herself to all the services that she was able to do for them.

4.   The Saint habitually did these charitable works out of her love for the Lord and with great compassion and diligence. She employed women who went out looking for the poor to bring them to her, and she received those people as if they were Christ himself. With a wonderful joy, they filled the houses in her street with those poor sick people. She herself served them and had others serve them with great love, never refusing anyone who came, because of her love for the Lord.

5.   All this service was carried out at Roubaud, where they looked after them with the utmost care and gave beds to all who came to them in the holy name of God. When she encouraged the others to do these good works, she would say fervently to them, "Do not think, my daughters, that it is men that you are serving. Rather, it is the person of Christ himself."

6. One time, as she was returning from the church, she met a poor man who was in a very bad state. As soon as she saw him, her heart was struck with a sword of amazing compassion for him, and when she arrived home, she sent someone for him. After seeing how ill he was and how he was suffering, with his head and his legs eaten by worms and his body covered in wounds, she was filled with emotion, remembering her poor Lord Jesus Christ, and for love of him she wanted to serve the man with special care. With great devotion she began to clean his wounds, to remove the worms and to wash his wounds, as she knelt humbly before him.

7. They lodged him in a house close to Roubaud and there they looked after him lovingly for three days, generously providing for all his needs. He did not want to eat in front of them, however, and had them place what they brought him on a window by the head of his bed. Each evening, after they had served him and put everything in order, the ladies would lock the door when they left, so that he could not leave the house where he was kept unless someone opened it. After they had looked after him in this way for three days, on the third night, after they had shut him in as usual, the good women who were sleeping in the house near the garden shed where the sick man was, saw a great light shining in the garden around midnight, and the garden seemed to be all ablaze as if firebrands had been lit.

8. All night they saw this light shining in the garden. In the morning, the women came to the door at Roubaud to get the key, wanting to look at the sick man. But when they opened the door, they could not find him anywhere, nor could they tell what had become of him. Immediately they had people look for him in all the hospitals and in many other places, but he could not be found.

9. They were completely filled with joy and amazement. On the window, they found all the food untouched. Although it had been there for three days, it looked and smelled as fine as if it had just been placed there. The first day's meat was as fresh as the last day's. It was not changed in any way.

10. In her charity, the Saint modeled herself on all she saw and knew of the saints, both men and women. For this reason, she can be compared to many of them, for she took up a virtue of each one. When she was urging those closest to her to increase their practice of holy virtues, she would sometimes tell when she instructed them, that she had never been told of any perfection of a saint that she had not taken up herself.

Chapter Nine

Chapter nine is about her diligence and fervour in prayer and about her raptures

1.   The Saint had acquired a gift for prayer through her marvelous practice of it; for she had always made a wonderful habit of praying, right from her childhood. It did not seem possible to her that anyone could serve God without it, and in every way possible she urged and cajoled the others to make a habit of it. Many times she told them, "You may be sure that as long as you continue in prayer, your institution will last, and you will persevere in all good things; but as soon as it disappears from your midst and you abandon it, I consider everything to be lost". "For prayer", she said, "is the bond and the guarantee of our institution."

2.   Prayer was her refuge in all things. It seemed as if she organized all her time and her activities around it. Her spirit had risen to such heights of thought that, to her, even eating and drinking were occasions for prayer. Very often when she was eating, she would be so drawn to God that she would forget herself and would stop eating. In every act of goodness and gentleness that she experienced, she contemplated and remembered God's supreme gentleness and goodness. And so, she would forget everything, even herself, in remembering her Lord.

3.   This holy woman was a shining example of the highest virtues, just as God's holy friend, Brother Hugh of Digne, had said about her and prophesied. He had said, "She is so devoted to our Lord that her gentle intellect can lead her mind only to great things." For although she was a simple, uneducated woman, Our Lord raised her to the most sublime heights of contemplation. Constantly giving her attention to heavenly matters for long periods of time, she would so frequently be with God in sublime raptures, as if she were in his presence, that she seemed to be leading the life of an angel among people, not the life of a woman.

4. She loved and sought out solitary places, so that she could be more completely with God. For that purpose, she had a secret chapel where she undertook to pray to Our Lord and to be close to God in prayer. She would water this place with her holy tears and would stay there in constant contemplation. As a result of this, the love that she had for Jesus Christ engendered new desires in her and from these secret desires she would become intoxicated with new ardour. She would be lifted above everything and transported out of herself.

5. She could not hear about God or Our Lady or Saint Francis or any of the Saints, men or women, without being moved to ecstasy. Many times she was caught up in such lofty contemplation that she would remain in a state of rapture for an entire day. Experiencing superhuman feelings in that state, she would be unaware of what was happening around her. This was verified many times with many testimonies by different people. Seeing her so caught up in these raptures, they would push her and shake her forcefully and even inflict pain on her, but they would be unable to move her.

6. Sometimes she would be suspended in the air, without supporting herself in any way. Her feet would not be touching the ground except for her two big toes. Supported by the strength of her amazing rapture, she would be so forcefully lifted up into the air that she would be the space of a person's palm above the ground. Many times people were even able to kiss the soles of her feet when she was in that situation.

7. One time, she was in the church in a state of rapture and a noble knight named Lord Jacques Vivaud, the lord of the castle of Cuges, was in that same church with his son, on the evening of a feast day, after the sermon had been delivered. And his wife, a noble lady devoted to good works, whose name was Madame Sanche, told him that the holy mother had been in a state of ecstasy since the morning, and that she herself had accompanied her into the Friars' chapel where she had received communion that day.

8. When the nobleman heard from his devoted lady that she was still in this state, he went to see her with great devotion. He saw her raised in the air where she remained suspended through the strength of the amazing attraction that she felt toward God. She was not touching anything and nothing supported her in any way. She was raised so high above the ground that the nobleman and his son knelt with great respect, removed their hoods, and very reverently kissed the soles of her feet. What they had seen filled them with wonderful joy and spiritual elation. They have since told many people about this, declaring firmly that this is just how they saw it with their own eyes, and that they kissed her feet with their own lips.

9.   Another time, a similar thing happened to Raymond of Puy, of the same city of Marseilles. He saw her in a state of rapture in the Friars' church in front of the altar where she had received communion. She was raised above the ground in the same way that the others had seen. Then this citizen knelt reverently and, with his hand, measured the distance that she was above the ground and he found it to be more than a hand's-breadth. Filled with faith, he put his whole head, which had been causing him pain, beneath her holy feet, and kissed them with great devotion. Afterwards he had no more headaches. His head was free of pain from then on, and he was very strong and healthy.

10.   In addition, he had a fistula on one of his eyes, which had been troubling him for some time, and he had been unable to cure it. But from that moment on, he was never afflicted with that illness and he was completely cured in a very short time.

11.   He also told people that, because of her qualities, God had been very gracious to him; for before the events happened that we have just been describing, there had been considerable discord between himself and his wife. There was so much strife between them that they were never able to be at peace. This was because some malicious person had done certain evil things in order to hurt them, so that they would not be able to get along and would separate from each other. But a short time after he had seen the Saint in her ecstasy, they were together very peaceably. And the person who had harmed them suddenly admitted to it after he went away. He returned from the church with his heart completely at peace because of what he had seen and that person revealed herself to them and undid what she had done to them. She herself was amazed to know how and why she had suddenly been changed from something that she believed she would never be rid of. But she felt such repentance that she could not rest until she had confessed it and had put it right. From then on, nothing like that ever happened to them. They lived many years in perfect peace and, because of his devotion, this noble man later placed one of his daughters in Roubaud.

12. There was also a lady named Beatrice, who had come from another country to serve God, following the example of the holy mother, to be part of her institution. She swore that she had measured with her own hands the distance that the holy mother was raised above the ground in a rapture that she had witnessed in the church of the Friars. It was on the feast day of Our Lady, after she had received communion in the chapel of Saint Cecilia. Her whole body was suspended in the air. One of her feet was a hand's-breadth above the ground, and only the tip of the big toe on her other foot rested on the ground. And she remained this way from the time she had received communion until evening, around compline.

13. Many other people observed how far she was above the ground in these ecstasies, and measured the distance with their own hands on different occasions. There were many who, when she was in this rapture, kissed the soles of her feet in devotion, in the same way that has been described above.

14. The certainty of her true raptures has been proven in many ways; for, some people who wanted more proof would stick awls[7] into her body and would prick her with needles, but she felt nothing and did not move.

15. Once, when she was in a state of rapture in the Friars' church, a person who doubted the truth of her ecstasy approached her and drew out an awl that he was carrying and cruelly stuck it into her. The holy mother did not move and did not feel it at all. But afterward, they found the bruises and cruel punctures that she had suffered. Later, when the Saint had returned to her normal state, she often felt severe pain and suffered greatly, although she did not complain.

16. The first time that King Charles saw her enraptured, he wanted to test if the ecstasy was real. This was at the time when he was count of Provence. He tested it in the following way. He had a quantity of

---

7 A sharp, pointed spike, the awl was a small tool used by shoemakers and others for pricking holes.

lead melted and had it thrown, boiling, onto her bare feet, in his presence. She felt nothing. The king held her in such affection because of this, that he made her his commother. But afterward, when she had come back from her rapture, she felt great pain in her feet and her anguish was unbearable. She was very ill from it and unable to walk.

17. When she returned from her heights of rapture, she would look sickly and weak. She would be kind to all the women, asking with curiosity about the affairs of the convent, and about their concerns, as if she had not just received some new grace from Our Lord. She would be careful afterward to maintain the appearance of a humble sinner, so that the memory of what had happened would fade from their hearts, and they would not believe it. For she did everything she could to hide the grace she had received from Our Lord, even from those who were closest to her.

18. For two entire years, she hid it so well that she kept everyone from finding out about her true raptures, until she was raised to such a high level of contemplation that she could not hide it from the women around her or conceal herself from them. For wherever she might be, when she heard God spoken of, she would enter a state of rapture. If she were at table, listening to the reading and heard any words of devotion, she would be caught up at once in rapture, right at the table, and would no longer be able to eat.

19. If she heard any sound that excited her devotion or gave her pleasure, she would be raised immediately to ecstasy. She could not bear any sweet sound, or almost any singing, not even the singing of birds, without becoming enraptured. Once, she heard a solitary sparrow singing and she said to her companions, "What a solitary song that bird has!" And then she was immediately in a state of ecstasy, drawn to God by that bird's singing.

20. So high and so amazing were her glorious raptures that there were times when she was so strongly held by them that she was unable to come out of them. The sisters feared that they might lose her in this way; for her body, which had been weakened by the long penitence that she had done, could not bear the spirit's great strength.

21. She would secure herself so completely and firmly in God that her body would almost collapse. When she emerged again, she would be so exhausted that she would have almost no physical strength.

When she reached this state, nature was left with no support and was not functioning in her. She could barely be revived, and seemed to have no life left in her. So great was the attraction that drew her to God that it overcame all her natural strength.

22. These raptures became so strong that she could not hide them, even from the lay people; for she had reached the point where she could not hear the mass or sermons, or receive communion, without being enraptured the whole day. That is why many people observed her, both seculars and nuns, countless people, both barons and prelates, even princes, kings, counts, and many others. These occurrences were so frequent and so prolonged that they could not be hidden.

23. Whenever this happened, she would remain at first just as she was, until the force that was drawing her would lift her up. And she would be held in this ecstasy, with her eyes raised to heaven and fixed on high, towards the one for whom she yearned.

24. Crowds of people rushed to see her and to look at her in that state whenever they managed to hear about it. Her face shone with such goodness that they would gaze at her as if she were an angel. The people, in their devotion, would be so eager to rush toward her, and even to touch her clothing, that they were often in grave danger because of the crush. No matter what the brothers or the sisters did, they could not prevent it. Even when she was in chapel with the sisters, after receiving communion, with the gates shut so that no one could get in, they would impetuously climb up on the gates. It was feared that the gates would be broken because so many people were climbing on them, trying to see her in her rapture.

25. She inspired such devotion in the people that sinners were converted to God. Seeing her in her ecstasy, their hearts were greatly changed. Certainly, the great comfort that people received from Our Lord at that time and the renewal that they felt in their soul when they saw the wonders that God was working in her, were definite proof that these were truly holy raptures, raptures that did not come from a feigned love, but from the fervent and extraordinary ardour that she felt for God and from a heavenly desire for the things from on high.

26. And because the holy woman was trying, as much as possible, not to reveal the secret gifts that she was receiving from God's goodness, she stopped attending sermons and convent masses in order to keep people from seeing her in that state. For the same reason, she stopped receiving communion on the high feast days. In order to be less noticed, she would receive communion on the eve of the feast day, in the early morning, right at dawn. She did it so devoutly that she inspired piety in those who saw her.

27.   Afterwards, she would always be in a state of ecstasy because, when she came to receive that holy sacrament, she would be consumed with love for this blessing in her fervour. That is why she did not remain in herself and was completely transported in her love. And so whenever she received communion, she would offer herself so ardently to God that it seemed as if she would faint with the great fervour of spirit that consumed her. She would be so drawn to God in these ecstasies that at times it seemed that she would not be able to come back from them, so firmly was she held by the one she had found.

28.   Sometimes it was so late when she came out of her ecstasy that they took her back to Roubaud by lamplight. For, when she was in this state, she would unite her soul so completely with God in love that she seemed listless when it was time for her to leave the rapture, as if all the bones in her body had been pierced. So great was her ardour that, to her, all this seemed to last less than an hour or an instant, for her soul was continually burning with that desire. And so, once when she was coming out of her rapture, she said very despondently, "*Meum modicum, meum modicum.*" ["Oh, how little for me! Oh, how little for me!"] And as she was saying that, her heart seemed to fail her entirely. For that reason, she did not want to take communion in the presence of the people, so that she could be more intimately with her Lord.

29.   When she found herself among people who were speaking about God and she felt the touch of the spirit's attraction, she would immediately try to escape from that place, hurting herself in some debilitating way, so that the love she felt for God would not be recognized. One time, a devout friar, who was the lector in the convent in Paris, came to Marseilles. He wanted very much to see the Saint and to speak with her, because of the good things that he had heard about her, for the sweet fragrance and renown of her holiness had spread far.

30. One day he came to see her and, speaking of Our Lord, the lector said to the holy woman, "Lady Douceline, what is the soul?" And God's Saint answered humbly, "Brother, it is not for me, a simple woman, poor in every respect, to answer this question." Recognizing her humility, the friar persisted even more in asking it.

31. And suddenly, the Saint's spirit was set aflame as she reflected on the words that he persisted in repeating to her, and she was immediately caught up in rapture, impelled and drawn by the force of the wonderful feeling that she had from the words that the friar was saying to her. And then one could see that her hands were all torn and bluish in places, because she had pricked them with needles under her cloak, so that she would not hear what the friar was saying to her. But such was the ardour of the spirit, with a strength greater than that of the flesh, that no pain that she felt in her body could take from her the feeling that she had for God.

32. When the friar saw this, he was filled with wonder and great comfort because of God's goodness. He left her in her rapture and went away praising Our Lord. Late in the evening, she was still in that state, when suddenly she rose up with great fervour. Her face became bright red and was all afire. And she began to answer the question, speaking with intense feeling. She said, "What is the soul? *Speculum divine majestatis* [It is the mirror of the divine majesty], and on it God has set his seal." This answer was reported to the great lector; upon hearing it, he said, "Truly, all the masters and all the teachers in Paris could not have given a better solution to the question."

33. When the count of Provence sent for her, because of the dream that his wife had, the countess was very anxious to see her in a state of rapture. So that this might be more likely to happen, she wanted to receive communion and asked the Saint to receive it with her. The holy woman, who shunned the world's glory and men's praise, told her humbly that she was not prepared to receive her Lord.

34. Then the countess had a good friar come to preach before her. He spoke most ardently about Our Lord. At his words, the Saint was immediately moved by a fervour of spirit and fell into a state of ecstasy, despite her efforts to do those things to herself that might keep this feeling from happening. She had so tortured her hands during the sermon that they were covered in bruises. When the countess observed this wonder, she rejoiced greatly in Our Lord. She summoned all her children, and made them kneel reverently before the Saint, with their hoods removed, and she made them kiss her hands. She remained in that state of rapture for a long time. And the countess, who was later the queen of Sicily, held her in great and special affection from that time on.

35.   But some people who wanted to be more convinced, tested her unscrupulously in painful ways. They stuck needles into her fingers, between the skin and the nail, to make her suffer more pain, so that she might move. But God's Saint was so attracted by the true and strong feeling that she had for Our Lord that, when she was in that state, she did not feel any bodily pain, however severe it might be. That is why she did not move, no matter what they did to her. But afterwards, when she came out of her holy ecstasy, she bore the marks of it and suffered great pain. Because of all this, the whole court praised God for what they had seen in her, and from then on they regarded her with extreme reverence.

36.   It happened that the count of Artois came to Provence. He was a very devout man, and when he heard people talking about the great holiness of that lady and about her raptures, he was moved with great piety and wanted very much to see her in that state. When he was in Marseilles, he went to see her, taking with him a few good friars who could speak well about Our Lord. And they began to talk about the stigmata of my lord Saint Francis, whom she loved very dearly, and about that sweet conversation that had taken place between the Seraph and my lord Saint Francis, when he was given his wounds.

37.   When she felt herself being affected by the words that the friars were saying, with humility, she began to torture herself secretly, beneath her cloak. Afterward, they found on her hands the marks and bruises that she had tormented herself so that she might escape that strong feeling and not hear what was being said. But it was all to no avail, for her spirit was so ablaze that no pain could extinguish her ardour.

38.   God's holy contemplative was suddenly so inflamed by those words that she fell into ecstasy. When the count saw her, he felt a great joy, because he had received what he so much wanted. Filled with delight, he rose at once, removed his hood and, as a sign of his respect, went forward on his knees from the door of the oratory to the spot where she was, and kissed her feet very devoutly. He was filled with great devotion for her and went away comforted and delighted, leaving her in her rapture.

39.   She remained in that state of ecstasy for a long time. Then, with all the sisters surrounding her, she suddenly rose up with great excitement and said joyfully, *"Letatus sum in his que dicta sunt mihi, in domum domini ibimus.* I was glad when it was said unto me that we will go into the house of the Lord."[8] Saying this, she opened her arms wide in the shape of a cross and rose so high above the ground that she seemed to be wanting to go up to heaven. And her face showed a wonderful joy. When they saw her rising up like that, they all went forward together confidently to stand beneath her arms, and they asked her whether they would be saved. Her face blazing with ardour, she answered them, "I tell you truly that beneath the wings of Saint Francis you will all be saved." It would be impossible to describe how great was the joy that they all felt on hearing these words. The consolation that they experienced was so great that it seemed as if they were with God.

40.   Later, when the Saint came to herself and came out of her holy rapture, she remembered that the count had been there and that she had been in great pain. She appeared to be so distressed that it would be difficult to tell and describe the suffering she displayed because the count had seen her in that state. With bitter tears, she said to them all, "Unfaithful sisters, why did you allow this? Why did you put me on display like that? How could you do such wickedness and betray me in this way?" After that, with bitterness of heart, she said to Our Lord, "Lord, I beg you to confound me in the hearts of each one." She seemed so upset that it was as if some great wrong had been done to her.[9]

---

8   Psalm 122.

9   Douceline's words here seem to echo those of her contemporary, Juliana of Mont-Cornillon. Unwilling to meet dignitaries who had come to visit her, Julian blamed the recluse, Eve of St. Martin for having sent them: "If I could hate you, recluse, and if I might do it without sin, I confess that I would! Were it not for you, I would never have been mentioned in the courts of princes. And whence do I deserve that bishops should come to me? [Luke 1:43] But I pray the king of the world that before my death, he may allow me to bear as much shame and disgrace as he has granted me reverence and honour, although unwillingly, because of their visit" (Newman 1991, 113).

41.   Whenever she felt or knew that strangers had seen her like that, she showed the same pain. That is why, in her distress, she gave orders to all of them as firmly as she could that, in accordance with holy obedience, no one dare to let her be seen, or show her to anyone, when she was in that state.

42.   She had an indescribable love for the blessed father Saint Francis. His name was always on her lips, showing that she was constantly remembering him. Many times when she came out of her height of rapture, she spoke of him, or of his poverty, or of the holy marks of Christ's wounds that the saint bore.

43.   Once, when she had been in a state of rapture in the friars' church, and had spent a long time in front of the altar where she had received communion, suddenly she moved away from that altar and, full of fervour, rushed to the altar of my lord Saint Francis, shouting out with ardour in a loud voice, "There he is! There is Saint Francis! His views will be severely attacked, but assuredly not with the truth. He will certainly win the day and be victorious. He cannot be defeated because, with the Lord's seal, he will frighten away all his adversaries. He is coming with his banner unfurled", she said, "Christ's standard bearer, carrying the seal of the sovereign king, with which he will strengthen the knights of the Lord's army, marking all those who will be his disciples. He will display the king's flag which he bears imprinted on his body, to encourage all the warriors."

44.   She spoke with a passionate delight, and with supreme joy in her heart and on her face. When she was talking about the standard bearer of Christ's army, my lord Saint Francis, who was marked with the holy stigmata, she could no longer control herself, and was immediately carried away by her emotion, because of the extraordinary devotion she had for Christ's keeper of the seal. After Jesus Christ and his blessed mother, she put her trust principally in him, ahead of all the other saints, and she wanted to be governed by his example. They frequently found her in a state of ecstasy, with the book in her hands, reading the saint's life. She urged everyone to be devoted to him; and in almost all her discourses, she would talk about Saint Francis.

45.   Each day, her spirit reached a higher level of contemplation in God. She could not listen to any singing in the church without being at once enraptured. That is why she attended only low masses, held in private. Every celebration of Christmas she spent with God in contemplation, because she could not contain herself of being suddenly ravished when she was reminded of the great blessing that day had brought. The memory alone would draw her to God. And so she would spend all of those days in a constant rapture.

46. One time, at Christmas, she wanted to receive communion at night after matins, at the midnight mass, because of her devotion to the hour that the son of God was born. She took communion secretly in a chapel of Saint Cecilia, where she was accustomed to doing it. And when she had received her beloved Lord, remembering how he was made a new man on that night, she felt such affection for that wonderful child whom she loved tenderly, that she went at once into a state of ecstasy. And she remained continually in that state all the rest of that glorious night and all of that blessed Christmas day. She spent that glorious feast day in a spiritual way, with the infant and his mother, and all day long she took no other nourishment.

47. When she returned from these holy raptures, she always spoke words of scripture related to the feast day or the blessings that it brought. And then she would be extremely happy, as much from the newness of her joy as from the ardour of her spirit. Her face, which previously seemed death-like from her long, severe acts of penitence, would be bright red and blazing.

48. Each year, on Holy Friday, she would be in a constant state of rapture the whole day and even into the following night. She would shut herself up in her oratory so that no one could see her, until the ladies sometimes forced open the doors and found her enraptured. Every year on that day, the emotion that she felt for Jesus Christ, as she remembered his suffering, would be so strong that she seemed almost to expire as she contemplated the Lord's passion and the Virgin's sorrow. Her face looked so exceedingly afflicted and tormented that it was hardly possible to look at her during that day when she was enraptured. She indeed manifested such affliction in these ecstasies of Good Friday that it was almost impossible to witness them.

49. On one of those days, she was in one of her raptures, weeping in anguish for the sorrow of the Virgin and her son. She cried loudly, in such bitter grief that it pained them all to see her so distraught. Her cries could be heard from a great distance. She had such compassion for the Virgin and was so filled with grief that it seemed as if she must die with her. It was evident from all the signs she showed and from her great sorrow that the suffering which Jesus Christ endured had been revealed to her. She felt it so strongly that it seemed as if every vein in her body was going to burst from the pain caused by what she had seen.

50.   With bitter cries she was saying to the Virgin, "Lady, see what they are doing to thy son, how they are wounding him and breaking his body, how they are treating him horribly and killing him." She was weeping with inexpressible sadness. Then she said that she could not go on. She was very weak and worn out with sorrow, unable to endure such torment. She remained like that all of that Holy Friday, and into the night as well, without eating or drinking. In that state she appeared to be truly dead.

51.   When the sisters saw that matins were being said and that the better part of the night had passed without her moving, they were very frightened because, looking at her, she did not appear to have any life left in her. So they called to her and shook her, but nothing they did could make her move. And she stayed like that till after the first hours of sleep. When midnight came, she began to move, but she was so filled with memories of that day that she did not know what she was doing and scarcely heard anything that was said to her.

52.   Then a lady arrived whom the Saint called her prioress and to whom she had promised obedience. This woman made them set the table and told her to eat. But she was so caught up in the blessed contemplation she had entered that she had forgotten all temporal things. And she asked what it meant to eat, for her soul was occupied with other things. The prioress commanded her to eat, saying that the table was set, that the day was over, matins had been said, and that it was time to eat. She said she wanted her to do it. And the holy woman answered that it was indeed true that the table was set and prepared for everyone, the table on which lay the lamb that had been sacrificed.

53.   And immediately she was in a state of ecstasy and she could hear nothing that was said to her, thinking only of that blessed table of the cross, toward which she directed all her attention. And when the sister who was her vicar told her to eat, she said that she was commanded to do this because of Christ's obedience on the cross. Then she fell back into her rapture. This debate went on so long that all the women were troubled. They could not make her eat, no matter what they said. She was so attracted to the cross that she did not give any other words in response except those mentioned above. And immediately she returned to her state of ecstasy.

54. When the night was almost over, they pulled and pushed her in order to force her to move, and with great difficulty they made her eat a little. While she was eating, they told her that a noble lady who was extremely devoted to her, Madame Mabilia de Gignac, mother of the Reverend Father Raimond de Gignac, had sent her a calf. As soon as the Saint heard this, she was reminded of the sacrificial calf, and that memory immediately put her into a new rapture. She remained in it all night, and nothing that they did could bring her out of it. When the next day came, she was filled with a spiritual joy, and busied herself with the affairs of the convent and with all her responsibilities, as if nothing unusual had happened.

55. Another time, on the same day, she had sent the women who were taking care of her to the church, and before they celebrated the cross they went to see if she needed anything. When they came to the door of Roubaud, and while they were still in the street, they heard the holy mother crying so passionately that it seemed as if her heart was being torn out. They rushed to where she was and forced open the door of the oratory where she had shut herself in. It was at the hour of the celebration of the cross. They went in and found her in a state of ecstasy, with her arms stretched out in a cross. She was so lifted up in her ecstasy that her feet were not touching the ground. With bitter sighs she was weeping loudly for the passion of the Lord. Her deep sorrow was indescribable and her anguish was just as if the sight were right before her eyes.

56. She cried out bitterly, *"Ecce lignum crucis* [Behold the wood of the cross]. Oh traitorous sinners, all the wine with which you make yourselves drunk comes from one pipe, and here are five wounds that flow like pipes for you! Untrue Christians! You are always getting drunk on a little wine and yet you don't know how to drink deeply from these five ever-flowing streams. A denier's worth of wine changes a man and transforms him so that he no longer tries to avenge the insults he has received; and yet these five wounds from which Christ's blood flows abundantly cannot transform a man so that he will not seek revenge for the insults he has received!" And it seemed as if her heart was breaking for Christ's agony.

57.   Another time, on Holy Friday, she was in a trance, and at the moment of the celebration of the cross, she rose up very high and began to cry out, with great tears and anguish, saying, "Oh false and deceiving world, what terrible punishment is coming upon you!" Then she said, "Come, come back, get into the boat, for anyone who is not in it will perish." And then making her voice stronger, she cried out still more loudly, speaking with all her strength, "Don't you hear the boatman crying? Don't you hear him shouting to get into the boat because anyone who is not in it will perish? And those souls are covered in the blood of Christ!" She was saying this with great emotion and bitter tears. Then one of the women asked her, "And will we be in the boat, Mother?" The Saint answered this question with great delight, "Truly, beneath Saint Francis's wings, you will all be saved."

58.   One Easter day, it happened that she was in a rapture in her oratory, and she was lifted up into the air, supported by the force of her marvelous ecstasy. One of the ladies measured with her hand the distance that she was above the ground and she found that it was more that a hand's breadth, and she was not supported by anything. Her face was ablaze with her ardour. With her spirit alive, she cried out, full of passion and delight, *"Quis est iste qui venit de Edom, tinctis de vestibus de Bosra?"* ["Who is the one arriving from Edom, coming from Bosra with his clothes stained with blood?"][10] And she showed such wonderful joy that it seemed as if her heart could not hold such happiness of spirit or the fullness of joy that her soul was receiving from God.

59.   On another occasion, on the eve of the Ascension of Jesus Christ, when all the sisters had gone to hear vespers, the holy mother remained behind. She began her prayers beneath a tree, praying to Our Lord and meditating on the holy day. When they returned from vespers they found her under the tree, enraptured. She remained motionless while they said compline and matins. When the bell of Salvaterra sounded the curfew and the ladies saw that she still did not

---

[10] Isaiah, 63:1. Verses 1 to 6 of this apocalyptic poem were frequently commented on by Joachimites.

move, they said that because of the dusk some harm could come to her if she stayed there, for she was suffering from very bad pains in her head.

60. While they were thinking of taking her to the dormitory, she got up and started walking ahead of them, standing up straight, still held by the rapture that possessed her, with her eyes fixed on heaven and her whole heart wonderfully drawn upward. But when she entered the dormitory, as soon as she found herself beneath the relics that were at one end (for they did not yet have an oratory in which to place them), she knelt before them still enraptured, and made a gesture of reverence to them. Then she stood up and began to sing, walking through the dormitory from one end to the other as if she were following a procession. When she had walked and sung a little, she stopped and listened. After she had listened for little while without walking, she answered and began singing again, moving along as she followed what she was seeing.

61. All the women who heard it found the singing to be wonderful. It seemed to come from another world, for no one could understand the sounds or the words. It seemed as if the singing was completely consuming her, right to the marrow of her bones. When she reached the end of the dormitory, she would turn around and make her way to the other end. She did this countless times, coming and going, singing in turn, as if she were part of a procession. The singing was of such sweetness that she became quite languid. It seemed to them at times that she was saying, "New Jesus, new!" At other times they thought she was singing, "*Nove Ihesu, nova Iherusalem, nova civitas sancti!*" ["New Jesus, new Jerusalem, new holy city!"][11] But they could not understand the truth of the words she was saying or catch the sounds.

62. All of them followed after her in procession, with lighted candles, accompanying her, full of joy and inexpressible consolation. The spiritual renewal that they all experienced, and the new feeling for God that they had in their hearts were so strong that they felt they were sharing in the delights of the heavenly court and were following

---

11 The new Jesus is Saint Francis and the new Jerusalem is the Church of the third age in Joachimite typology.

with her in that wonderful procession that they believed she was seeing in heaven.

63. When they saw what she was doing, they all understood that great things had been revealed and made evident to her in her rapture, things concerning God's sublime majesty. For she was giving visible signs of it, showing with her right arm, in a remarkable way, that she had seen the sovereign power of God: when she stopped, she raised her arm as high as she could and made a circle around her head with wonderful solemnity, using the whole length of her arm to indicate the diadem of God's great magnificence. The respect and the authority that she was indicating by this grand gesture was so extraordinary that they were all frightened by it and felt a great respect for the Lord that she was representing to them.

64. Having seen the signs that she was making, they were firmly convinced that God, in the presence of all the saints, was giving a blessing to that house. It was in fact the time when the house of Roubaud was being built and settled in Marseilles, and the dormitory had been recently constructed. She remained in her state of rapture until after the hour of matins. Her face was wonderful to see then, and they looked at it with delight, because of the heavenly brilliance that shone in her eyes and the spiritual joy on her face.

65. Once, on the day of Pentecost, returning full of enthusiasm from the rapture she had been in all day, she was full of fervour, in a spiritual intoxication and was speaking in a very animated way, telling how God the Father had given his gifts to the holy apostles on that blessed day, and had bestowed his noble gifts upon them, making them drunk with his Holy Spirit which the Son had promised them. She spoke warmly about that good wine that cannot be confined or kept from spreading abundantly everywhere, intoxicating everyone who tastes it. It seemed that she herself was intoxicated in her enthusiasm, full of fire, and her heart seemed unable to contain such an overflowing of spirit. It seemed that she had tasted the wine she had been speaking of and was drunk with it.

66. And she was saying wonderful things about the knight who had acquired that gift for us at the cost of his blood that he had shed for us, and who had conquered his mortal enemy with his own weapons. She was telling how he had defeated him with his nails and with the lance of Longinus that pierced his own body and how he had triumphed on the cross where he vanquished all his enemies. She said many other glorious things of lofty meaning that could not be understood or comprehended, but she spoke with strong feeling and supreme fervour.

67. Another time, she was in the convent of Hyères on Christmas day. She received communion at early morning mass and from that moment on, she was in a state of rapture until evening. When she came out of her rapture, late at night, she was saying joyfully, *"Puer natus est nobis et filius datus est nobis."* ["Unto us a child is born, unto us a son is given."][12] She was singing this sweetly, with such joy and energy that she was no longer in control of herself and was filled with gentleness for the tender infant. The friars were around her, listening devoutly and reverently to the holy things she was saying, and she was speaking gloriously about the holy blessing of the incarnation.

68. Then one of the friars, who was the lector in that convent, asked her, "Lady Douceline, tell me how God speaks to the angels and saints in Paradise when he has no mouth or tongue?" And the Saint, very animated, answered with a full heart, "Brother, this is how God speaks to the angels and saints: when they give their attention to Him, they see and hear everything that God wants to say." Impressed with this answer, the lector said that all the teachers in Paris could not have answered the question better.

69. On the feast of Our Lady in mid-August,[13] she had received communion very devoutly in the same place early in the morning, and as usual she remained in a state of ecstasy all day. And when it came time for compline, she rose up very high, so that her feet were a hand's breadth above the ground. While the friars were saying the compline, she left the altar where she was and went from the chapel of Saint John to the altar of the Mother of God, which is in front of

---

12 Isaiah, 9:6.
13 The Feast of the Assumption of the Virgin on 15 August. The German mystic, Elisabeth of Schönau, in a vision which she experienced on 15 August 1157, was assured that "our Lady was taken up into heaven in flesh as well as in spirit". She had put the question to Mary "because, as they say, what is written about this in the books of the fathers is found to be ambiguous." Elisabeth's manuscript, *The Resurrection of the Blessed Virgin*, circulated widely. See Clark, 210; 294 n. 265.

the choir of the church of the Friars Minor of Hyères. There she
bowed to the Holy Virgin, and the friars started singing the
antiphony. Then, in front of the altar of Our Lady, the holy mother,
lifted high in body and soul, began to sing excitedly and with joy,
"*Assumpta est Maria in celum, gaudent angeli.*" ["Mary has been
taken up into Heaven; the angels are rejoicing."][14] And there was
marvelous great joy on her face.

70.   Then all the friars responded together to what she had sung,
abandoning the antiphony and showing the spiritual elation they
were all feeling. The Saint then entered the friars' choir, singing
fervently of the assumption of Our Lady. And the friars joined her in
what she was singing, with inexpressible consolation. And she
moved along like that, lifted up in the air, not touching the ground,
with the whole choir of friars singing beyond the grille. She was still
in her rapture and seemed to be following the procession that the holy
angels made to the Virgin Mary when she went up into Heaven. With
respect, the friars followed behind her very devoutly, supporting her
with joy and veneration.

71.   Another time, on the feast day of Our Lady, she was in a state of
rapture at Hyères, in the sisters' convent. And after she had been like
that for a long time, she began to sing the praises of the Virgin,
befitting the feast day, with enthusiasm and with delight on her face.
Then she began to speak fervently and joyfully about the glorious
round table where all must come to sit down. And she was saying
wonderful things about that table where people were receiving the
perfect food.

72.   Now, one of the novices, who was very devoted to her, asked
her, "Mother, mother, will I be at that table?" And the holy mother
answered her very lovingly, "Yes, my daughter, you will ultimately be
there." The young girl was deeply comforted by her promise, firmly
hoping and trusting that it would be as she had said.

73.   The wife of the lord of the castle, who had a share in the
domain of Hyères and whose name was Huguette de Fos, did not
believe what was being said about the Saint, and doubted the reality
of her holy raptures when she heard people taking about them, just as

14 Hours of the Virgin, Lauds. See also chapters 9:74 and 13:6.

Jerome, the noble cleric, had doubted the sacred stigmata that Saint Francis had received from Jesus Christ.[15] And she wanted to observe her in her state of ecstasy. On the middle day of August, she went to visit her, bringing with her the good friars who would speak impressively and devoutly about the assumption of the Virgin Mary. Upon hearing what they said, the Saint began to contemplate the great glory which the holy Virgin, the mother of God, received on that blessed day, and at once she was enraptured.

74. When she had been like that for a little while, she began to come out of it, singing joyfully, *"Assumpta est Maria in celum, gaudent angeli, laudentes benedicunt dominum."* ["Mary has been taken up into Heaven, the angels are rejoicing, praising and blessing the Lord."] And she sang so sweetly that it seemed to come from the mouth of an angel. When this unbelieving woman saw and heard this, she abandoned her unbelief, and from that time on she was extremely devoted to her and always had the greatest respect for her, because she had a profound change of heart at the sight of her holy rapture.

75. These true raptures were very frequent and were verified by many people who bore true testimony to the splendour that came from her eyes and that her face was like an angel's. They told how they had recognized the truth of it and had seen the marvelous things that happened on many occasions when she was in her holy raptures, which were very real and highly miraculous.

Chapter Ten

Chapter ten deals with the steadfastness of her contemplation, with the revelations that she received from God, and with the constancy of her resolution.

1. Among the other favours that God, in his bountiful goodness, had bestowed upon his humble servant, my lady Saint Douceline, was this: that whenever she began thinking about God, she would suddenly forget all this world, even herself, so that it all seemed insignificant to her. Her own body was forgotten, for nothing temporal would hinder her and no earthly thing would interest her.

15 Habig, 743.

2. So there was nothing that troubled her heart when she gave herself to prayer. She placed all her affection and desires in God, and fixed her mind entirely on him. And on those occasions when she had to deal with the affairs of the convent, once she had completed the business, she would turn again to her praying. And if anyone happened to observe her afterwards, they would find her in a state of rapture. On one occasion, she had spoken with one of the sisters about a very serious matter and had given her opinion; and when the other woman went back to her a moment later, she found her already fully absorbed in her praying.

3.   She told her confessor that it was through the Lord's generosity that she had received this grace, and that when she went to pray, it was as easy for her to put things out of her mind, without any effort or difficulty, as it was to remove the veil that she wore on her head. After her death, Friar Jaucelin, the bishop of Orange, told of this in his sermon to the people. He was the one the Virgin had given to her to be her director, at the time when she appeared to her after the death of the Saint, her brother. She comforted her in her deep sorrow and sent this friar to her, from whom she could take counsel. This man knew more about her secrets than anyone else, and after her death he revealed some of these things. He was her counselor, approved by the mother of God; and there was a special affection between them. The Saint had promised to obey him in order to make herself more virtuous and to acquire more worthiness in everything.

4.   One cannot say enough about her resoluteness. She was as steady as a cornerstone or a column, for she was founded firmly on the solid rock that was Christ. That is why nothing could make her change her good resolution. After her death, her confessor revealed that, from the time she was given to God, there was never a time in her whole life when she thought of doing the opposite of what she had set herself to do.

5.   From childhood she had wanted to serve God with purity. And so she rightly deserved the visits and consolations of the angels. Because she tried diligently to imitate the life of an angel, the Lord often comforted her with visits from them. Many times, the holy angels visited her as their friend. They kept her from any evil and gave her an abundance of good things.

6. It was also demonstrated and proved by sure signs that great secrets of God's wisdom were revealed to her in prayer, although she did not reveal this or communicate it to others, except when the love of God compelled her to do it or when it was to someone's benefit to do so. That is why she revealed certain things to her confessor.

7. The Saint was in the habit of reciting the hours to God and of saying her office with great devotion and reverence. Although she was afflicted with a great deal of physical suffering, yet, she did not lean on anything when she recited the office of Our Lord; rather, she held herself upright, without looking around, so that she might render to the Lord, with her mouth and her heart, everything that she ought to.

8. Once, in Advent, she was saying the matins of the blessed mother of God, and when she came to pronounce these words: "*Ecce ancilla domini.*"] ["Behold the handmaid of the Lord"],[16] she was suddenly very agitated and said, "There is the mother of God right there!" Having said this, she fell to her knees, kissing the footprints where the Virgin had passed by. And she stayed a long time on the ground in a rapture brought about by the supreme devotion and love that she had for the mother of God, from whom she received many favours; and the Virgin made herself well known to her.

9. One time, a pious countess had a dream about her, which she related to her husband. She saw an oil that was very pure and sweet and clear, like gold, flowing from the holy mother's breast. It was being burned in a beautiful, gleaming lamp, in front of the altar of the blessed Virgin mother of God. This represented the purity and fervour of her prayer, and the outcome of it. Her praying was pleasing to God and to the Virgin, and was worthy of being answered, for her holy prayers were very fruitful and benefitted the people of this world.

10. It happened once, on Christmas eve, that she was in her oratory, spending the night in prayer, when she felt the sweet anointing of the spirit come over her and she was transported out of herself and was filled with sublime thoughts. And when the hour of midnight came, at the moment when the true God and true man was born, she began,

16 Luke 1:38.

with great affection and emotion, to reflect upon the birth of the son of God, and to think of how he was born in purity from the holy body of the Virgin Mary. As she was engaged in this devout contemplation, her spirit was suddenly transported through God's grace to the place where the Virgin was, and she saw, openly and clearly, the precious mother of God. A ray of sunlight was coming from the womb of the holy Virgin, and at the end of the ray she saw the child.

11.   On another occasion, in the renewal of the fullness of time, she was shown a manger where the Virgin mother put her beloved son, among lilies; and he was receiving nourishment from the Holy Spirit, who was radiant with the intensity of his love. And the manger was transported with the son and the mother to a place where rivers of delight were flowing, surpassing the understanding of men and angels.

12.   And another time, a hill was shown to her, higher than all the other hills of this world. It was round, and flattened on top. There was no path or road by which to climb it. The top of it was circular, as if it had been made with a compass, and around it there was a fence of lilies. Those who were living in this glorious place had been brought there by the Holy Spirit, and from there they were taken before the majesty of God where they sang continually, "*Sanctus, sanctus, sanctus, dominus deus exercituum.*" ["Holy, holy, holy is the Lord of Hosts."][17] Within the girth of the hill there was a circle surrounded with lilies. Here alone was the queen, the mother of God. Those who lived on this hill, who wanted to pray to the Virgin, came by a very narrow path to the enclosure there. No one was allowed within the enclosure except she to whom Our Lady was accustomed to grant her many comforts and favours.

13.   Whenever she was in the church, she felt her heart drawn to the tabernacle where she knew the sacred host of the precious Lord to be. For the good Lord would draw her immediately to himself, and her love would, at once, turn her towards him. Her whole heart would be lifted up in great devotion to God. Once, when she was in the church, with her mind lifted up in thoughts of the respect owed to the sacred tabernacle in which the holy sacrament was enclosed, she was seized with a warm love for Jesus Christ in the sacred host. Overwhelmed

[17] Isaiah, 6:3.

by these lofty thoughts, her soul was transported into the tabernacle where she experienced incomparable delight.

14. While she was joined in this union with the sacred host through her sincere love, she saw clearly the sacrificed Christ, unclothed to his waist, his hands crossed on his chest, and his face full of goodness. He was very pale and covered with bruises, and there were wounds in his hands and side. Filled with emotion, she said, "Lord, how is it that you are like this?" And he answered with sadness, "Those whom I love, and have loved so much, my own friends, have treated me like this."

15. Her confessor recounted that, on another occasion, when she was in the church of the Friars Minor in Marseilles, she saw the open tabernacle where the Corpus Christi lay. And with her body's eyes she clearly saw Jesus Christ in the tabernacle, completely overcome, bleeding from all parts of his body, and gravely wounded. There was still fresh blood flowing from his wounds as if he had just been taken down from the cross. She looked at him with deep sorrow in her heart, weeping bitterly and moaning heavily. In her grief she asked him, "Ah, Lord! who did this to thee?" Jesus Christ replied, "The traitors seated at my table."

16. At the time when the holy father, Brother Hugh, passed from this world, the holy mother was inconsolable and extremely distressed. So she turned to the Mother of Grace, as a refuge, asking her to direct her and to take care of her and her daughters, for whom she was very concerned. And the Mother of God, full of gentleness, appeared to her with exceptional kindness, and gave her great comfort in her distress. For certain people were trying to destroy the holy institution that the Saint and she had founded, saying that such a fragile establishment could not survive, and advising her to embrace another order.

17. Then God sent her a holy Friar Minor whose name was John of Parma, a truly holy man.[18] At that time he was Minister General, but later he gave up the office and retreated to a mountain for a long period of penance. He lived a remarkable life and possessed a great spirit. Led by the will of God, he came to Marseilles after the death

---

[18] John of Parma, 1209–89, Minister General of the Friars Minor 1247–57.

of the Saint, while the holy mother was experiencing the difficulties that were preventing the growth of her institution. The holy woman was delighted at his arrival. She took his counsel concerning what would be pleasing to God, and told him of her intentions.

18.   When the holy man learned all about the holy institution and how it had begun, and when he knew her intentions, he was filled with the spirit of God and, raising his hand, he placed it on the Saint's head, saying with assurance, "My daughter, remain committed to what you have so successfully begun; do not try to do anything else; you have no need of another order. Do not remove yourself from the situation in which God has placed you, for you may rest assured that the Lord has set you there."

19.   She said that, upon hearing what this godly man said to her, she felt a firm conviction take root in her heart and mind, and that since that time, no matter what happened to her, she was not daunted by anything, and from that time on, nothing deterred her in her intentions for the holy order. She always remained steadfast, as if the hand of God was supporting her. She had felt that the holy man was speaking through the inspiration of God's spirit. And her mind was at rest in Our Lord and she gave thanks to God, for it had pleased him to give solace to her poor spirit.

20.   From then on, the order began to grow. And when people would often say that, after her death, the institution would perish, the Saint would reply vehemently, "Certainly not; for God is the guardian of this holy establishment." "In truth", she would add, "I would be willing to die, so that people might see what God has planned for this poor and humble institution, and so that you might see how it will last forever, by the will of God." And she always showed herself to be very confident in front of the other sisters. She found comfort in Our Lord through a vision that God sent to her.

21.   One time at Hyères she had spent a long time in a state of rapture. In that state, as her confessor later recounted it, she saw a ladder, all made of gold, that stretched from Heaven to earth.[19] A great multitude of angels was going up and down on it, and when

---

[19] The image of Jacob's ladder is a recurrent one in the visions of medieval mystics; see, for example, Elisabeth of Schönau (Clarke 68, 148).

they came before the majesty of God, they knelt down and bowed before the Holy Trinity. And then she was assured that the three persons of the Trinity guaranteed her institution and were guarding and protecting it.

22. And when she came out of that rapture, they recognized that her heart and her face were remarkably changed, for she appeared to be amazingly calm. Then she called the sisters together in chapter and spoke wonderful words to them in a great sermon, urging them to be grateful to God for all his kindness and favours, and to be faithful to their religion and to their order which would continue to be strong. And speaking publicly to them, she showed that she was convinced it would carry on after her death, saying that she would not hesitate to give her life to ensure that it would always exist.

23. "It is certain", she said, "that the service of God will always be carried out in this place." She was completely convinced and had no doubt whatever. "The Trinity is assuredly taking care of this holy order", she said. She spoke at such length and with such passion that they listened to her in amazement. She was so filled with God that she did not seem to be in control of herself. So they believed that she must have seen great things that people are not worthy to know, for she appeared to be filled with wonder.

24. Afterward, she ordered that, in each of the convents, they practice daily a devout remembrance of the Holy Trinity, because she said that they were all under the Trinity's protection and guardianship. So she ordered that each day, at the conclusion of matins, which ends the night and ushers in the day, they should all reverently repeat the antiphon of the Holy Trinity, all standing together, and then all bowing together, kneeling down, recite it in an orderly fashion, and then they should say the verse and the prayer. After compline, they should do the same thing, for it was the last hour of the day. They were at all times to give thanks to the Trinity for having protected them.

25. When the holy mother was encouraging them to have a fervent love for their holy institution, she would speak passionately to them, "My daughters, stay united in the love of the Lord, for you are joined together in the love of Christ. He has bound you together in his love. All the other orders have a rule that holds them firmly together, but your only bond", she said, "is love. This little cord alone, the love of

Christ, keeps you together, because it is a stronger bond than any of the rules. The love of God that has held other orders together with a strong rule, is nothing more than that same love of God which by itself binds all of you together. The Lord has put a knot in it which cannot be undone, so that you are all joined in his love. Who can separate you from his love? I assure you that in the whole world you cannot find as strong a rule as this which has tied you so well and so firmly together; for there is nothing that can separate you from the love of Christ".

26.   Once, on Holy Thursday, after she had been in prayer, she remained full of fervour and, in a spirit of devotion, she was able to speak profitably to the others. And when it came time to carry out the holy ceremony of the washing of the feet, the sisters assembled in an orderly way, as they were accustomed to do on that day. The holy mother was among them, an example and mirror of contemplation and a model of profound humility and perfection.

27.   Before the ceremony, she began to speak with extraordinary passion, urging them all to spend the holy day in deep devotion, meditating on the cruel death of their merciful Lord. She told them their hearts should be heavy with the memory of his passion. And she encouraged them to feel it in an appropriate manner by telling them of an example, one that she herself had been told by Our Lord, of a good man who wanted to know how he should conduct himself on Good Friday. It pleased God to show him what he wanted to know.

28.   On that Holy Thursday, a dove came to him and did nothing unusual all day, until the evening. But when evening came, the dove appeared to be suffering; its wings began to droop, and it bent its neck and lowered its head to the ground. It seemed sad and very sick. As night came, and as the day of sorrow neared, it seemed to become worse. But on Good Friday, at the ninth hour, it collapsed to the ground as if it were dead. Its wings were spread out, its neck drooped as though it were broken, and its head rested on the ground. Lying on the ground, it appeared to be dead. From then on, it stayed like that all day and all night, and gave no sign of life.

29.   When Holy Saturday came, it revived and appeared completely renewed, lively and happy. It spread its wings and flew high into the air. "We should follow its example", the Saint said, "and be pure and simple of heart, like the dove. On that solemn day, we should show that we are stricken with grief and terrible sorrow for the suffering of our merciful Lord and stay in a deadly sadness, until we learn of Christ's resurrection."

30. For some time, the holy mother's mind was preoccupied with a great concern for her order. She wanted with all her heart to find a way in which the institution that she had founded for the glory of God could be left unified and held together in the love of God after her death. This was her ultimate desire. Her great concern was to determine how it could be done in a way that would be pleasing to God. So she devoted herself entirely to prayer, humbly asking to know God's will.

31. It happened that, when she was at Hyères, she spent a long time in a state of rapture, and when it was over she seemed particularly comforted. Filled with divine inspiration, she called the sisters together in chapter and, with great kindness and affection, she urged them all to make it their heart's desire to maintain the unity of their holy order. She told them that it had long been her wish and her fervent prayer to Our Lord that he would let her know how the order might be permanently kept together after her death. And by the will of God, it had been granted to her to know that it was God's wish that there would always be one sister, chosen by common consent between the two convents, who would keep the holy order together. With humility and by her holy encouragement, she urged them to carry that out.

32. They each came, one after the other, to lovingly make a vow, with their hands between hers, to preserve forever the unity of that holy order in the way that she had told them: which is to say that after her death, they would all be bound for all time – those who were living then and those who would come after – to elect, by common consent and in the love of God, one person whom all the sisters in the order would be bound to obey humbly, so that their unity would never be broken. And as soon as that person died or was excused, they would elect another. She had them all make this vow in each of the convents.

33. When she had led them humbly and with holiness to accept what she wanted, so that they would all be held together in the bonds of unity, and when she saw that those good things she desired had been accomplished, she was filled with an indescribable joy. Intoxicated with the spirit, and with her soul overflowing with a wonderful affection, she pronounced the most generous benedictions upon them. She poured out a blessing upon the holy order, and she gave God's blessing, and that of the holy father, Brother Hugh, and her own to all those who would faithfully keep their vow and lovingly preserve their unity.

34.   She was extremely anxious to preserve the order, and she often heaped great blessings on those who, by their life and by their fine example, drew others to the convent who would greatly benefit it, and who would help to maintain and preserve that poor and humble institution, to the best of their ability.

35.   She would say, "From the mouth of God, and from his mother, from the blessed father, the lord Saint Francis, from all the Holy Trinity, and the heavenly court come blessings upon all those who persevere and keep this holy institution flourishing. Let my blessing and the blessing of our holy father, Brother Hugh, be given to them. There is no doubt that those who carry on and who live their life according to the order's counsel will all be saved beneath the wings of Saint Francis; for a special grace has been given to Saint Francis and special consolations are kept for anyone who will faithfully follow his counsel and that of his order. That is why, if we are resolute, we can hope to enter surely the kingdom of God with them."

36.   On the other hand, she spoke most severely about God's curse that would fall upon the heads of those who, by their wicked lives and their bad example, would lead others to evil. She assured them that God's terrible anger would come to them. In a frightening way she cursed all those who would destroy the purity of that holy order, or who would disrupt it by their evil actions. "From the mouth of God", she said, "and from the Holy Virgin, from Christ's standard-bearer [St. Francis], and from our holy father, Brother Hugh, who counseled our order, and from all the saints, will come curses upon anyone who breaks up our poor and humble institution or who brings about its dissolution."

37.   She would become extremely annoyed if anyone said that the establishment would die without her, and that it could not last. She would react to what was said, telling them that God had not done any of this through her, but that the Lord himself had been the principal founder and settler of the holy order. It was he who was its special guardian and defender, along with his mother, his standard-bearer, and the holy father [Hugh]. And it was absolutely clear that God would preserve it, as he had already been doing.

Chapter Eleven

Chapter eleven tells of her understanding of the Scriptures and of her spirit of prophecy.

1. Through her constant attention to prayer and her remarkable practice of virtue, this humble servant of Christ had reached such clarity of thought that her deep reflection had led her to an understanding of the Scriptures, although she was otherwise not well-educated. Sometimes the Friars would confer with her about the Holy Scriptures and ask her questions. Inspired by God's spirit, she would give such profound and clear answers that the most learned among them would be amazed.

2. Once, one of the order's renowned teachers, who was in Marseilles, asked her some particularly difficult questions. God's Saint answered him so confidently and with such clarity and insight that, even though the man's learning had led him to a different understanding, he recognized readily and openly that what she had said was right. And then this great man admitted that, because of her contemplative spirit, the Saint's understanding surpassed his own, even with all his learning. Afterward he told the friars about this, with great admiration.

3. The spirit of prophecy shone in her as well, because of the level of contemplation that she had reached. And so she saw things that were not evident and knew what would happen. She understood what was in people's hearts and advised them about these things, to the benefit of their souls.

4. At the time when King Charles was count of Provence, the pope proposed, at God's command, that he take the kingdom of Sicily.[20]

---

[20] According to Runciman, the pope had first offered the crown in August 1252. Charles, on his brother's instructions, refused it. In the spring of 1262 the throne was offered to King Louis; he refused it but this time allowed his brother to

But the count was uncertain about how to proceed in this matter, which all the kings had rejected. Because of the love and respect that he had for the Saint, he asked her advice about it.

5.   The holy woman encouraged him strongly, saying that he should not hesitate to accept this undertaking which had been offered to him by the will of God. She told him he should not be afraid of anything, because the Lord wanted to make him the champion of his Church. She said he could be sure of victory and would triumph, with the help of the Lord and his mother, and of Christ's standard-bearer, my lord Saint Francis. But she told him that, after those things that God would do for him and through him, he should be careful not to be carried away with pride, as the first king of Israel had been in his ingratitude. For if he did that, God would reproach him as he had done to Saul when he took his kingdom away from him.

6.   Having received the Saint's advice, the count decided to accept the undertaking, urging her to pray for him, secure in the expectation of the victory that she had promised. And indeed he proved to be victorious over the enemies of God's Church, and gained control of the kingdom, just as the holy woman had predicted. And once he had clearly recognized the Saint's spiritual nature and the truth of her words, his devotion to her and his respect for her only increased.

7.   On a number of occasions the Saint informed him, and let him know in her letters, that God was not pleased with him and that he was preparing to punish him. She said that the Lord had still more sticks in his garden that he would use to chastize him, and that if he were not careful, he would be severely punished for the sin of ingratitude; for God would let the weight of his powerful hand fall on him. She informed him about many secret and confidential matters, and the king was amazed that she was able to know these things.

8.   Many other times, she told him in advance of things that would happen to him. And it always turned out as she had predicted. Even the end of his reign came about as she had said it would, that as long as he feared God, all his affairs would turn out well and God would accomplish great things for him. To the end of her life, the Saint took

proceed. By late July 1263 Charles had become the Church's official champion (72–86).

care to remind him of this. She would often tell him in her letters that she greatly admired the wonderful things that God was doing through him, but that she feared he was not showing gratitude for it, and she assured him that, if this were so, it would cost him dearly and he would suffer serious losses because of it.

9. A short time later, after the Saint had died, he forgot about fearing God, and before long he found himself under attack from the king of Aragon and his brother. They waged a terrible war against him that brought him great troubles.[21] His son was taken prisoner and held in strict captivity.[22] This misfortune brought him such pain and sorrow that he lost heart; he died ruined and stripped of his kingdom.[23]

10. A young woman who was very devout came to visit the Saint. She comforted her with kind words, and urged her to love her creator and to reject all the pleasure of this world. She told her, "You have everything you want and enjoy it, so you think that, because you have a young husband, you will never lack for anything. But be sure that you will need to try hard to have a great deal of patience, because you are going to need it."

11. The lady took these words to heart and could not forget them. It was not long before her troubles began, and she immediately recalled what the Saint had told her would happen. She became convinced of the truth of her predictions, because after that her husband caused her much unhappiness for a long time. And she said that, during those difficulties, the fact that God's friend had warned her of them in advance had been very helpful to her.

12. Once when the holy mother was spending some time at the convent of Roubaud at Hyères to support the sisters there, a young

21 At the hour of vespers, on Easter Monday, 1282, the population of Palermo massa-cred the French garrison in the city. Massacres of the French all over the island fol-lowed. Charles of Anjou raised an army to crush the rebels but the Sicilians offered the crown to Peter of Aragon. Peter landed with a strong army in August 1282 and the ensuing War of the Sicilian Vespers dragged on for 20 years. According to the terms of the final settlement, the house of Aragon kept the island of Sicily and the Angevins kept the territories in the south of Italy, with the title "king of Naples". See Runciman.
22 His eldest son was Charles of Salerno (d. 1309).
23 Charles of Anjou died 7 January 1285 at the age of 58.

lady was staying at the castle. She was in secular clothes, planning to live her life in the outside world, as her parents and friends wanted her to do. Now it so happened that on Pentecost she went to the church of the Friars Minor at Hyères, where the blessed mother was experiencing one of her raptures. The young lady had never seen her before, but when she heard people talking about her, she wanted to join her community, although she had never considered it before.

13.   By God's will, she entered Roubaud where the Saint herself put the robes on her. And she loved her so devotedly that she would have wanted never to be away from her. She constantly wanted to be assured of her love, because she felt that if the Saint loved her, no harm could come to her and she would be loved by God. One day the holy mother spoke to her privately and encouraged her by telling her what she so much wanted to hear: "Thou may rest assured, my daughter, that I love thee among all the others." As proof, she mentioned a kindness that she had done for her. And because of other things that she said to her, the young lady was sure that God had revealed his heart to her.

14.   Another time when she was alone with her, she wanted to get her permission for something that would give her some comfort, but she was embarrassed to ask for it. Without her saying anything, the blessed mother recognized what she wanted, through God's spirit, and gave her the permission she was looking for. And on another occasion when she was in her presence and was wanting to hear some words of comfort from her mouth, the Saint looked right at her, and laughed and told her what she wanted. It made her blush to know how clearly she could see her thoughts and wishes. That is how she recognized that she had the spirit of prophecy.

15.   A young lady, 12 years old, had entered Roubaud, but she was tempted to leave the convent and to secretly abandon the sisters' order without telling anyone. One day, she went to the door, determined to leave and to return to the world. The holy mother sensed her temptation and thwarted it by calling out her name and telling her to come to her. Putting her arms warmly around her, she said, "Be firm and confident, my daughter." And placing her hand on her head, she said, "Don't be afraid, my child, for Saint Paul says one who is not tempted will not be crowned." And from that moment, her temptation was gone and it never troubled her again. She led a good life and ended her days in that holy order.

16.   There was another woman from Marseilles, whose conscience had been bothering her for a long time. One day when she was alone with the Saint, the holy mother spoke clearly to her about what was troubling her soul and the woman was amazed that she knew about it. Shamefully she admitted her guilt to her. The holy mother reprimanded her severely for keeping it in for so long and not wanting to reveal it, and she gave her wonderful guidance for her salvation. Then she gave her gentle words of comfort for the distress that she had been in and consoled her so well that she was never again troubled about it. It was through God's spirit that the holy mother knew the secret that the woman had not wanted to reveal.

17.   One of the servants of Roubaud once happened to go in the company of another woman to a castle where her family was. Upon her return, the holy mother scolded her harshly, saying that she knew how she had behaved and what she had done there. She even told her some things concerning her conscience that the woman had not wanted to reveal to anyone.

18.   Another day when she happened to be in prayer in the church, one of the members of her community who was nearby started to think about an issue of holy obedience concerning something the holy mother had not allowed her to do. She wanted very much to do it but, remembering that the Saint had not permitted it, she did not dare to keep considering it. While she was thinking about this, the holy mother turned to her and, in response to what she was thinking, granted her wish.

19.   Another time, she was in her room with another sister, speaking words of piety and wisdom to her, when the sister began thinking about other matters. Immediately the holy mother looked directly at her, and told her with a smile what she had been thinking. The sister was astonished, and with shock she admitted that it was true.

Chapter Twelve

Chapter twelve is about the miraculous things that God did through her.

1.   God distinguished his poor and humble servant, my lady Saint Douceline, in many ways, filling her with the highest virtues. She had reached the height of her perfection; and the truth of her saintliness and the certainty of her exemplary life was evident in the following miracles.

2.   In the town of Hyères there was a child who was suffering from an illness that made him lose the natural use of all his limbs, so that he was quite helpless. The child was brought to the Saint, who was moved by their humble pleas and by the prayers of the sisters and of other good people who had come with him. Out of compassion for the boy, she touched him with her hands, and immediately he was healed and healthy, and recovered the use of all his limbs.

3.   At the time when the sisters were living by the Roubaud River, at Hyères, a man who was living there, a notary by the name of Fouque de Ramatuelle, came and asked the portress to have the holy mother come to the door because he wanted to see her. He had brought with him a horse that was dying. Although she did not know why she had been called, she went to the notary and found him with the animal. He pleaded with her humbly and tearfully to touch the horse that he feared was near death. Moved with pity and compassion, the Saint was willing to grant his tearful request. The horse was very sick, but when she touched it, it was immediately cured and made healthy.

4.   A nun from the monastery of Almanarre, named Madame Huguette Blanche, had suffered for a long time from a serious ailment that had paralysed her hand and deprived her of its use. One day she happened to be at Hyères at the same time that the blessed mother was at the convent, where the community still is at the present time. The nun knew about her saintliness and so, when she heard that she was there, she believed that, because of her virtuousness, God would grant her the grace of curing the ailment that made her stiff hand useless.

5.   So she came to Roubaud and asked to see her. At the time, the Saint was in a state of rapture in the oratory or in the cell of one of the sisters, and had been in this state for some time. The nun pleaded with them to take her to where she was ravished. And when they did so, she touched the Saint's hands and stroked them with great faith and hope; and her hand that had been useless was cured, and she never again had anything wrong with it. She told different people about this miracle, and how she had been cured through the Saint's virtuousness. And she was able to use that hand as fully as the other one.

6. When the sisters were still in their first location at Roubaud, a noble lady from the family of the lords of Puget, named Madame Rixende du Puget, had come with her daughter to join the holy mother's community and serve God. She drew several other women of that family there as well, and they all did very fruitful work. This sister was afflicted with a serious eye ailment, and very respectfully she begged and prayed the sister who was serving the Saint and looking after her, to keep the wine that was left in her cup after she had drunk from it. The sister washed her eyes with this wine very reverently. After bathing her eyes with the wine that the Saint's lips had touched, she was completely healed and cured of the ailment she had.

7. Another woman with a serious affliction that she had had for almost two years was healed in the same way. She took some wine that was left in the Saint's cup after she had drunk from it and, after washing with it, she was cured of the illness that she had thought was incurable.

8. In the convent at Marseilles, a young beguine from Roubaud was seriously ill. Her feet, legs, and abdomen were so swollen that it seemed as if her skin would split. She could scarcely get out of bed, and could not walk around. In that convent at Marseilles, the sisters performed the ceremony of the washing of the feet on Holy Thursday. The blessed mother was there with them and in her compassion she wanted to wash the feet of this one who was sick. And when she had washed them and kissed them very reverently and affectionately, the young sister was cured of her illness and restored to health, although the doctors had given up and considered her to be dying and beyond being saved.

9. One time, the holy woman was going to visit the church of Saint Catherine which is in the city. On the way, she met ten or twelve men who were fighting with swords, trying to wound each other. When the Saint saw this, she shouted out three times, "Mother of God!"; and the hatred and anger in the men was dissipated and they went away at once, without hurting each other.

10.   In the city of Marseilles there was a widowed lady whose name was Mathiève. She had a three-year-old son who was born deaf and mute. He was so deformed that he had never been able to walk and people would stare at him because of his deformity. He had a hump on his chest and on his shoulders, and was all curled up. His toes were joined together and his hands were clenched. Some of his bones were dislocated and out of their place. In addition to all that, his head was eaten with fistulas, and he had such terrible lesions from them that the dressing they put in them penetrated to a depth of three fingers.

11.   It had reached the point that the sores were eating into his skull, and one of his ears was so eaten away with the disease that it was barely attached and hung down on his cheek; they expected it to fall off at any time. His whole cheek was affected, and even his neck. And the smell that came from it was unbearable. The child's father had died and his mother was extremely distressed. She prayed constantly to Our Lord to take him, because he was in such pain and source of more and more tears.

12.   One night she was instructed by a revelation from Our Lord and she heard a voice that said three times to her, "Woman, take the child and carry him to Roubaud. Have him touched by Douceline and he will be healed by the power of God." When it was daylight, the mother carried him to Roubaud, asked to see the Saint, and showed her the source of her distress. She told her about the disease that he had on his head and showed her his ear that was about to fall off. The Saint saw the lesions on his head and smelled the strong odour that even his mother herself could barely tolerate.

13.   When the holy mother saw him, she was moved to tears with pity and said, "The Lord has the power to do whatever pleases him. It would be nothing for God to heal this child, if in his goodness he wanted to do it." In her compassion and pity, she put her hand on all the diseased parts of his head. And as soon as the Saint touched him with her holy hand, the lesions began to heal and the dressing began to come out of the wounds; the diseased places took on a fresh red colour as if they had been healing for three or four days, and there was no more odour.

14.   His mother was amazed when she saw this, but she was afraid to let it be seen that she recognized what had happened. She showed her how the child was bent and his limbs all stiff, and she had her touch them with devotion. The Saint was moved by the sight of the child's disabilities and she was filled with pity for him and extremely moved. With tears streaming down her face, she held his feet and his clenched hands that he had never been able to open. As soon as she did this, his hands began to open and he stretched out his fingers and toes.

15. Then the mother showed her that his mouth was clenched shut and he was unable to speak, and she told her child, "Open your mouth." But he did not hear her. Then the holy mother said to him, "Open it, in the name of Christ." At these words, he opened his mouth wide enough that his mother was able to put the Saint's finger into it and had her touch his tongue and his whole mouth so that she could see that he was not able to speak.

16. Continuing like that, with a remarkable faith, she had her touch the child in all the places where he was disabled or deformed. The holy woman was so filled with the goodness of God for the child that she hardly knew what she was doing. She was completely drawn toward Our Lord, and she said to the mother, very compassionately, "Truly, it is easy for God to be merciful and to show his goodness to this child; nothing is beyond God, if it pleases him." Then, weeping profusely, the mother asked for her prayers with great devotion, and went away carrying her child.

17. When she arrived home, she put the child where she usually kept him, tied and wrapped up. All day long she didn't know what else to do. As she was talking with a woman who had come into her house, the child stood up by himself and moved toward his mother, fully healed and standing up straight, through God's power. When he was near her, he called out happily, "Mother, mother!" The mother was amazed and bewildered, saying that it was not her son, because she had heard him speaking. The woman who was with her asked if it was Pellegrin, for that was the child's name. He answered that it was, and said that the one who had put her finger in his mouth had cured him.

18. The mother took the child and examined his head and found all his wounds closed and amazingly healed over. His whole head was in such good condition and all the places where the flesh had been rotting were so restored that it seemed as if it had been healing for more than a week. And the ear that she thought he was going to lose, because it was barely attached when she last saw it, had been put back in place as securely as if nothing had been wrong with it. There was some stitching on it that looked as if it had been done with a needle. By God's will this stitching always stayed there as a sign of the miracle. It too was reddish and appeared to be recently healed.

19.   The mother was completely shocked when she saw the miracle. Weeping with happiness, she ran in amazement to her father's house, shouting like a madwoman, with the child following behind her. The father and everyone there who had known what her son had been like, realized that it was a miracle. To be more convinced, they touched his head and felt it with their own hands. They all looked at him as if he were a wonder, because they found that there was nothing wrong with him any more, and he was in perfect health. Amazingly, his twisted body had been straightened out and his deformities were gone.

20.   They all stared at this miracle that had just happened and joyfully praised God. The lady's father stood before them and said with great respect, "This woman is truly a saint for God to have done such an amazing miracle through her. This is something that should be made public and not kept quiet", he said. "I don't believe a more holy woman is to be found. Who would not want this to be made known? Go quickly, my daughter, and take the child to her so she can give him her blessing."

21.   The mother took her child with her and went to Roubaud. She showed the sisters the little one that they had seen all crippled, but who was now completely well. They all rejoiced to see him cured. But they cautioned the lady not to appear to believe that the holy woman had done this miracle, because she did not want to be honoured, and would not allow it. Then they took her with her child to where the Saint was. The delighted lady showed her the miracle, saying, "Mother, behold God's great goodness and mercy that have healed my child."

22.   When the Saint saw that he was cured, she was completely and wonderfully swept to God. With tears in her eyes, she gazed at the child and told his mother to give thanks to God and to Saint Francis, and to promise to make him a Friar Minor and, in sincere devotion, to promise him to the Saint. A long time afterward, the child's mother gave sworn testimony to this miracle, in the hands of the Friars, before she died. It was confirmed by the friars, by the sisters of Roubaud, and by other lay people. This took place at the time when her son was a priest and a preacher in the Order of Saint Francis. He himself was present and received into his own hands his mother's oath testifying to the miracle.

23.   In the same city of Marseilles, there was a woman who had suffered for a long time from a paralysis in her legs. The art of medicine could not heal her. Nothing that the doctors advised her to do was of any use or benefit to her. When she heard about the miracle that had happened to the child, she had faith that, if the holy woman touched her legs, she would be cured. So she asked insistently to see her, and when she came before her, she showed her infirmity. The Saint had pity on her and, as she looked at her legs, she touched them with compassion, and the infirmity went away; within three days she was completely cured, without taking any medicine.

24.   A poor woman had an only son who was suffering terribly from scrofula in his neck, and was wasting away with it. He had had the disease for a long time and it couldn't be cured. She brought him confidently to the Saint, explaining to her what his problem was and how poor they were. The Saint took pity on them and in a very kind way looked at the disease that the little one had on his neck. While she comforted the mother with gentle words, she touched his neck; and immediately the scrofula dried up and he was cured.

25.   Madame Nicolette Arnaud lived in the same city. She had lost all her children before they could be baptized. She had such terrible pain that she almost died trying to deliver her children and could not carry them to term. It would be impossible to describe how much sorrow this caused her, particularly because she had not been able to have them baptized. But she believed that if the Saint prayed to God on her behalf, she would find favour with him. So she came to her and explained her affliction and respectfully asked her to pray for her. As she was leaving, she most confidently placed the holy woman's hand on herself, despite her strong objections. From then on, she did not suffer the pain she had had before, and was able to deliver each of her children without difficulty. They were all born healthy and were baptized and all of them continued to live.

26. One day the holy mother happened to be looking at the convent's flour barrel and noticed that it was almost empty. In a grumbling way she said, "There is no more flour." She was surprised to find so little of it. When morning came, the sister who looked after the convent's provisions wanted to bake the day's bread. She went to the barrel with two other sisters who had been with the Saint the day before when she had looked into it. They found it full of flour, although when they were with the holy mother they had left it almost empty. They were overjoyed and very surprised, and went to report this to the Saint. She ordered them not to tell anyone about it, but to give thanks to God and Saint Francis. They firmly believed that God had done this miracle in answer to her prayer, because she had spent a long time in prayer after seeing the shortage.

Chapter Thirteen

Chapter thirteen is about her death.

1. Because of the Saint's advanced age and the long, harsh penitence that she had practised, her body was frail; nevertheless her heart burned with the desire to do still more, for she did not feel that she had yet done anything.

2. Her spirit was not dampened by the frailness that she felt in her body; in fact she became more energetic. As her body declined, her enthusiasm grew stronger. She was full of determination, as if she was starting out fresh, and she did everything she could to leave a better example for the others. For that reason, she did not spare her tired body or surrender to her frailty. As a result, the blessed mother's life was an example to all of them, until the time when it pleased the Lord to call her from this world into eternal life, when she was about 60 years old and had reached the height of her perfection.

3. Near the end of her life, her raptures were stronger, more profound, and more frequent, and her praying was more intense and constant. The nearer she came to the end of her days, the stronger her devotion became and the more intensely her soul burned for God. She had reached such an exalted state that whatever she saw or heard or felt drew her through contemplation to God. All that separated her from him was the partition of the flesh.[24]

---

[24] This phrase is reminiscent of a passage in the Life of Beatrice of Nazareth: "Her

4. She had such a deep and strong attachment to Our Lord that she seemed to have no thought for this world. When she was at table for meals, if someone brought her a flower, a bird, a fruit or anything that gave her pleasure, she would immediately pass into a state of rapture and be drawn up to the One who had created these things. Nothing could disturb her when she was like that, because the grace of the Holy Spirit had filled her completely and the love of God had set her entirely ablaze and purified her. Consequently nothing tainted with the love of this world was left in her, only a constant passion for God and a boundless, intoxicating love.

5. On the feast of Our Lady, in mid-August.[25] before she gave up her soul to God, the holy mother had taken communion the previous day and had stayed enraptured in front of the altar as usual. She was so deep in her rapture that she remained there all day, from prime until vespers had been said.

6. When the hour came for the friars to begin the vespers of the blessed mother of God, she was completely absorbed in God, even more than usual. And just when the officiant intoned the first antiphony that says "*Assumpta est Maria in celum, gaudent angeli.*" ["Mary has been taken up into Heaven, the angels are rejoicing"], she suddenly rose up into the air so high that it seemed as if she would keep on rising. That is how intensely she was wrapped up in God. The sisters who were around her were acutely aware of what was happening, and when they saw her rise up with such force, they were afraid that her soul was going up to God and that they were being left with only her body.

7. Then they all rushed toward her, crying out in the hope of holding her back, because they loved her tenderly and were terribly afraid of losing her. It is not surprising that such a mother would be dear to them, because when she was on earth, she was part of the glory of God; even while living in the flesh, she was celestial.

---

body, like a thin membrane which is easily broken or like a shining cloud which is easily penetrated by the clear radiance of the sun, seemed to obstruct her spirit which was always aspiring upward. . . . Therefore she implored in prayer that this thin membrane be speedily broken, and with fervent desire of the heart she persistently longed for the light little cloud to be driven away by the ray of the eternal sun" (De Ganck, 231).

25 The feast of the Assumption, 15 August 1274.

Because of the strength of the extraordinary attraction that was being exerted on her soul, her face was glowing and wonderfully ablaze with a spiritual fire, and her eyes were bright and shining. Everyone gazed at her in amazement.

8.   When she had recovered from this remarkable rapture, around the time of compline, they noticed a great transformation in her; she seemed changed in every way, even in her outward appearance; her face was unusually beautiful, like an angel's. And she was still so engrossed with Our Lord that she seemed to have completely forgotten this world. And then, from that point on, they realized that she was being constantly pulled away, and that she was barely aware of anything that they were doing to her. Her spirit was so completely absorbed in that love that it was as if she were suspended in God. They were convinced that, in this marvelous ecstasy, wonderful things were being shown to her that mankind is not worthy of knowing.

9.   They also believed that she knew then when her life would end and death would take her, because they heard her say something about it in an indirect way, which led them to understand that this had been revealed to her. But the tender love that she had for them kept her from speaking directly about it, for they were extremely fond of her, and they seemed to find it unbearable when they heard her talking about it. She did it in that way so that she could leave and go unhindered to her Lord, because her desire to be fully united with him forever was completely consuming her. Furthermore, she had set aside all other earthly love. There was nothing holding her back.

10.   When the eighth day came, a constant fever was holding her in its grip. She said to one of the sisters, who had come from a distance to visit her, "Do you know that the Lord acts like a mother feeding her child? She holds in her hand the piece of food that she wants to give to the infant and when the child is not paying attention, she puts it in the mouth. This, she said, is what the Lord will do." From then on, she declined daily, and the doctors said they could do nothing more for her. The force that was pulling her to God was so strong that her whole body was consumed by the fire in her soul. She was so ablaze with God that her body was completely collapsing.

11.   When the sisters heard this, they were overwhelmed with grief and wept copious tears, begging God to restore the holy mother. They did many things to save her: she had taken ill on Wednesday, and on Friday almost everyone in the convent practised the discipline of flagellation, crying out to God to restore her to them; the next day, Saturday, they fasted with bread and water, kneeling on the ground, in honour of the Virgin, humbly begging her to bring her back to them.

12. But her soul was so firmly joined to God and united with him that she could not turn back. Yet she could not leave;[26] for three days and nights she was in a constant state of ecstasy before she died. The doctors had told them that would be how they would lose her. The friars who had come to see her remained constantly with her all day. And when all hope of a physical cure was gone, they said to her, "Lady Douceline, to whom do you leave these women?" She answered, "I leave them to God and to the Order." Then they asked her. "But to whom do you entrust them?" Again she answered, "To Our Lord and Saint Francis". Then, when they asked, "Lady, whom do you leave in your place?" she answered, "The Holy Spirit will see to it."

13. The sisters wept bitterly, feeling as if they had been pierced with a sword of grief. Filled with great sorrow, they stood round her, watching her die. When the friars saw how distressed they were, they asked her reverently to give them her blessing. So all the women knelt together in their grief, and the holy mother stretched out her arms in the shape of a cross and blessed her daughters, both present and absent, in the holy name of Christ. She asked Him to look after her whole order. Then the only thing she did was repeat to herself, "*In te, Domine, speravi, non confondar in eternum*" ["My hope is in you, Lord, that I may not be confounded for eternity"], and "*In manus tuas, Domine, comendo spiritum meum*." ["Into your hands, Lord, I commend my spirit."][27] Having completed everything she had to do, this saintly soul went joyfully to her rest in God on the seventh day, ending her life still in that ecstasy that had lasted for three days and nights.

---

[26] This state of liminality at her death reflects Douceline's life as a beguine, situated between the lay world and the cloister, just as the tip of her big toe remained on the ground during her levitation (9:12).

[27] Psalms 30:2 and 30:6.

14.   The night that the Saint passed from this life, the main gate of Roubaud was not closed to anyone. A great crowd gathered as soon as they heard of her death, and so the whole house was full of people wanting to touch her. Meanwhile, the sisters were in a frightful state, as if they were dying from the weight of their tremendous sorrow, for her death had pierced their souls like a sword.

15.   The friars who had been there at her death kept watch over her all night, and did not leave until they had completed all the ceremonies. They took charge of the house and directed everything. The sisters of Sion were there as well, keeping watch all night, and many other devout people who mourned with the sisters and wept bitterly with them because God had deprived them of the holy mother's presence. They declared their belief that she was a Saint before God.

16.   When morning came, the news of her death was announced. As soon as people learned of her passing and the word had spread through the city, everyone was anxious to see and touch the holy body because of their devotion to her. Those who were able to take something that belonged to her, took it to make a relic of it. Some touched their rosaries and rings against her, and others their hoods.

17.   They even came with knives to cut up her robe and divide it among them.[28] Out of their great devotion they took everything of hers that they could. It was feared that they would ravage the holy body before it could be removed intact from the house of Roubaud, for they cut up all her clothing, and the friars could do nothing to prevent it. One of the friars almost lost his arm trying to protect her from them.

18.   Consequently they could not conduct the burial because of the crush of people. So the brothers discussed it among themselves and sent for the magistrate, so that he could have the holy body guarded by the servants of the court. The magistrate came immediately, along with the other authorities and dignitaries from the city to honour her and pay their respects; and they brought the guards of the court to protect her.

---

[28]   An implicit reference to the soldiers dividing Christ's garments, following his crucifixion (John 19:23).

19. Everyone joined the processions, both laity and clerics. They took countless candles and torches and justly praising her, they lit them to honour the holy body. They carried her with great ceremony into the church of the Friars Minor in Marseilles. The reverence and respect of everyone, both common people and nobility, was beyond description.

20. In their passionate devotion to her, all the common people rushed to the body, and the guards could do nothing to prevent it. Before they entered the church, they had put three tunics on her and each had been cut to pieces one after the other. Even when one of the friars spread his cloak over her, the people immediately cut it up too. Three times during the procession the sheet covering her had to be replaced. They left nothing that was put over her; everything was cut to pieces.

21. The guards, who were protecting her with swords and clubs, were barely able to keep the people from tearing her body apart in their great devotion, so it was extremely difficult for them to carry the holy body to the church in a proper manner. It was the most important men of the city who carried her, out of their great respect for her.

22. Very reverently they put her down in the same spot where the holy father, Brother Hugh, had first been placed. The friars honoured her for three days, coming in procession to the holy body each day to praise her, chanting with joy yet with reverence the responses and antiphonies of the office of Our Lady. The Saint was honoured in every way by the clerics, especially by the Friars Minor, who regarded her as a sister, and indeed in Christ she was the true daughter of the lord Saint Francis.

23. At the time when the Saint passed from this life, she appeared to one of the sisters, a kind expression on her face. Joyfully she said, "Do not weep for me. I am not dead, but have passed from this world to my father; and the one who suffered on the cross for me has taken me into himself." And at that, she disappeared.

Chapter Fourteen

Chapter fourteen tells about transferring her remains.

1. The honoured mother, my lady Saint Douceline, passed from the ruin of this present life in the year of the incarnation of Jesus Christ 1274, on the first day of September, a Wednesday, in the evening, around the hour of compline; on the Thursday morning her holy body was laid in the ground. Both lay people and clerics paid their respects to her; rich and poor gave her the highest honour, showing how extremely devoted they were to her.

2. And the Saint began to shine through her miracles, for large numbers of sick people came with great faith and reverence to her place of burial and there, because of her worthiness, they received the healing they had been seeking. Many people with different kinds of illness were cured when they turned to her for help. Many came to her tomb with images, candles, shrouds and many other kinds of offerings to fulfill the various vows they had made when they had received the favours they had asked for from God, through her intercession.

3. In the year of the incarnation of Jesus Christ 1275, the friars and all the orders of Marseilles came together to transfer the body of the blessed mother, my lady Saint Douceline, with all the respect and praise that were due her. Her faithful daughters kept watch over her all night and guarded the body of their beloved mother, remembering her with a great deal of weeping and the intense emotion befitting the first anniversary of her death.

4. A rich man from the city, by the name of Guillaume de la Font, asked to look after the celebration, because of his strong devotion. And he did it most suitably. Torches, candles and other kinds of lights were lit. And there was great solemnity, with the joyful singing of hymns and spiritual songs of praise.

5. The body was borne reverently under a rich cloth of gold, and was taken in a grand procession and placed in the marble tomb that the rich man had had made for her, in the former church of the Friars Minor of Marseille, where the offices were being celebrated at that time. The entire celebration was carried out reverently and with the greatest solemnity and respect.

6. Some time after that, there were some troubles and disagreement in the convent at Marseilles over a certain expression in praise of the Saint. It had to do with the record of her life, at the time when it was first being written. The problem arose as a result of some doubt that had come to light. The sisters were at odds over whether to use the laudatory term [of Saint] or not. There was bitter turmoil among them, with some wanting it and others opposing it out of apprehension. The enemy of all that is good began to influence the heart of one of them; because she was upset and saddened by the conflict among them, she began to entertain a foolish thought.

7. It suddenly came to her mind that the Saint might not be a saint and not worthy of this term of praise. No matter what she did, she could not get this idea out of her heart, although she resisted it as much as she could. Still, by the will of God, they agreed to honour the Saint as they should. Here is what happened in that period of concern about her praise.

8. A novice who was devoted to her had been greatly affected by the conflict over the term of praise and she, like the other sister, had been very upset by it. One night, the novice was so ill that she was in bed, unable to move, and because of her illness she missed matins. All the others were well aware of it but no one dared to summon her, knowing how sick she was.

9. As the last call to matins sounded, while she was sleeping, someone came to her and began to pull on the cover that was over her, and woke her up. Then when she was awake, it was pulled again. She did not dare speak or ask who it was, because she was frightened of the spirit that she felt near her but could not identify. The holy mother was constantly on her mind. Having the memory of her in her heart made her exceptionally calm and took away the other fear. Nevertheless, no matter what she did, she could not move because of her illness.

10. And then, the one who had been standing in front of her left and went to the foot of the bed and began to pass her hand gently over her feet beneath the cover. Still, she could not move but the gentle touch on her feet gave her such pleasure that she forgot her illness and felt nothing but the pleasure that her soul received from it. When the other person saw that all this did not enable her to move, she lifted up the cover to expose her feet.

11.   At that moment, an antiphony in praise of the Saint came to her mind and all at once it was in her heart, as if someone was saying to her, *"Ad te de luce vigilans."* ["To thee I watch from the morning light."]²⁹ Suddenly, she got up without difficulty and found herself completely cured of her illness. The spiritual delight that filled her heart and the increasing devotion that she felt in her soul at the words *"Ad te de luce vigilans"* were so extraordinary that her spirit was comforted as it had never been before. In her joy, she went to say matins. But as she turned to go, she saw a person moving away from her.

12.   At that point, the sister who had had the foolish idea about the Saint was still in the dormitory on her way to matins; with her own eyes she saw a beguine moving away from the spot where the young lady that we have been speaking about was standing. She took the person for someone else, and was about to scold her, for she had called her. When she saw her measured pace, she looked to see who it was but she did not recognize her.

13.   She stood erect and was of average build. She seemed to have her arms folded in front of her in a cross, but her hands were covered by the robe that she had on. The veil that she wore was sparkling white and clean, and her robe was an unusual shade of brown.³⁰ She was extremely beautiful and astonishing to look at because her form was so perfect. She was walking through the dormitory very sedately, moving toward the oratory.

14.   The sister watched her as she came in front of her, but despite all her efforts, she could not distinguish her face, although she was looking carefully right at her. She was greatly surprised, because she knew that there was no woman like that in the convent. Then she passed close to her and when she was right by her, she asked who she was, because she did not recognize her. And immediately she had the answer in her heart: *"Dulcelina hec de Digna, Sede polorum est digna Inter sacras virgines."* ["This is Douceline of Digne, the one who is worthy of a place in Heaven among the holy virgins."] And then she passed on by.

²⁹ Hours of the Virgin, Lauds, from Psalm 62:1.
³⁰ The clothing worn by the ladies on the road to Hyères had been all black with white veils (2:4).

15. At that moment, she saw the shape of her shoulders and clearly recognized her build. The joy and spiritual pleasure that she felt in her heart at this answer and the deepening of her devotion were unlike anything she had felt before. She hurried to follow her immediately, and as she was watching her, she disappeared before her eyes. But she saw her go out through the door of the dormitory and thought that she had gone in through the opposite door, the one which led to the oratory and through which the sisters went to matins.

16. As soon as the figure had gone out of sight, she ran quickly after her and asked everyone where the woman was who had come in before her and where she had gone. The others answered that they had not seen anyone but her; and she was so elated that she did not seem to be herself. They all entered the oratory together, and once inside they experienced such glory there and they all felt such heavenly comfort and spiritual renewal that words cannot express it.

17. There was a celestial fragrance that they had never before experienced, and it seemed to them that the whole chapel was filled with angels. Soon after, the novice who had been ill that night arrived completely cured. She came in cheerfully, in wonderful spirits, and asked the others who had called for her. They all denied having called her; then she told them what had happened to her.

18. Because of all this, their happiness, far from diminishing, kept growing in all of them. It was a divine joy and a spiritual delight that had entered their souls, and with it came an increasing devotion to God and the Saint. This joyful bliss was beyond anything they had ever experienced. It showed on all their faces, a sign of the glory they were feeling in their souls. They took pleasure in looking at each other, because each of them seemed to see on the faces of the others what she was feeling in her own heart.

19. Then, they were able to see openly into each other's conscience, and were of one mind in thinking that the holy mother was there among them as they looked into one another's hearts as if into their own. They felt a part of the Saint's grand glory and sensed the presence of the holy angels that accompanied her. That is what they believed about this experience and how they understood it. In this joyful mood they said matins very devoutly, with candles lit to honour the Saint more fully.

20.   All the while that they were saying the nine lessons of Our Lady, they felt her presence there, and at the daytime matins as well, until the second nocturne. They were not able to see her, but they heard her quite close to them, coming and going, and could tell when she moved toward them and away from them. The joy in their hearts kept growing, and lasted all the time she was there, until some other people made some noise. As soon as the noise was heard, they felt her leave the place.

21.   Immediately, the increasing joy that they had felt in their hearts was gone. From that moment on, they no longer felt it, and were not aware of that same great glory. They all understood at once that she had gone from them, and they finished the service reverently, reciting her praises. And they remained for a long period of time in Our Lord's great solace, so that the memory and recollection of that day was sufficient to comfort them.

22.   The sister, whose thoughts about the Saint had been wrong, realized her mistake. She recognized that what she had heard was in answer to her mistaken idea that she might not be a saint and not worthy of praise. For the answer she heard was *"Dulcelina hec de Digna, Sede polorum est digna, Inter sacras virgines.* This is Douceline of Digne, the one who is worthy of a place in Heaven among the holy virgins."[31] So she repented of her error and was in great sorrow and anguish over the foolish things she had thought. And she was firmly convinced of the truth of those words.

23.   This happening was accurately reported to the head prioress and the elders of the convent by the women who had seen and experienced it. To be more convincing, the one who had that thought about the holy mother and who had seen her with her own eyes, swore on the holy Scriptures to what has been described here. She gave her word in the hands of my lady Philippine Porcellet, who was the head prioress of the community. And the others who had been there corroborated and confirmed that they had indeed experienced everything as she had told it.

24.   A similar thing took place in the other convent at Hyères a year later. It happened on the day that the sisters of that convent were

---

[31] Unusually, the Occitan original repeats the Latin phrase in translation here, as if to stress its great importance.

honouring the memory of the holy mother, as was their custom. They were carrying out their acts of remembrance with as much solemnity as possible, reciting her praises with great rejoicing. Their chapel was brightly illuminated with the various torches they had lighted.

25. They recited her praises with such reverence and devotion that they received a greater comfort than they had ever known. They had never practised such solemnity. Their voices could be detected even beyond the friars' street. People easily understood from outside the great solace they were feeling there, but were surprised at such a degree of solemnity, not knowing the reason for it. The joy that the sisters were finding in this new ceremony was not like an earthly joy, for they were seeing and hearing extraordinary things.

26. Some of the sisters who were the most virtuous clearly saw the holy mother come in to matins, entering by the sanctuary and going to stand in the midst of four sisters who were at the lectern. There was so much light around her that they were all illuminated. Several of them heard her sing for a time. The whole convent felt a strong sense of devotion to her, such as they had never felt before. When the sisters went to recite the verse, she followed them, and then disappeared. But the heavenly joy and the comfort and devotion that she left in their souls were immeasurable.

27. There is no reason to fear that Our Lord might abandon anyone who perseveres faithfully in this institution, or that he would not recognize them at the end of their days. To assure them all of this, God wanted to prove it to one of the sisters of that community.

28. It so happened that one of the sisters of Roubaud died in the convent at Hyères. Now, another one of them, who had been by herself in prayer, fell asleep. It seemed that she was in the same place as the soul of the woman who had died. She saw her lingering there humbly, in a place that seemed like an earthly paradise. And she saw all the Saints, one after the other, come to that soul and ask who she was, what order she was from, and what the habit was that she was wearing, because they did not recognize it.

29. She answered with humility, saying that she had been under the direction of Saint Francis. Giving her answer back to her, the Saints said, "You have been under the direction of Saint Francis!

Then why are you not wearing his habit, or the habit of Saint Clare, or one of the other orders?[32] Who are you, then, you who say you are under Saint Francis's direction and yet do not wear his habit? Who are you, and to what order do you belong?"

30. At that moment Jesus Christ appeared, the just and merciful Lord, and put an end to the questions by saying, "What are you asking?" And the Saints said, "Lord, this is a soul that we do not know; we cannot tell what order she is from, and we do not recognize her habit. She says that she has been under the direction of Saint Francis, but she is not wearing his habit, nor that of Saint Clare, nor of the other orders. She is not from a convent and we do not know who she is."

31. With his face full of kindness, the Lord answered softly, "I recognize her; she is from an order that I love, an order that is in my care and under the direction of Saint Francis. She is telling the truth when she says that she is under his direction, although she does not wear his habit. I know who she is." Our Lord said this and rescued her, taking her with him like a sheep for which he had paid a high price. So there is no reason to fear that this holy order governed by Saint Francis will perish, since it is constantly under the protection of Our Lord.

32. We have indisputable testimony and a sure guarantee of this in the holy mother's entire life, because at different times in her life, and in her most sublime periods of rapture, she promised us and assured us all that we were guarded by God and that the whole order is under the protection of the Holy Trinity, and that we will all be saved beneath the wings of Saint Francis. These were the things that she promised us frequently. And God wanted to demonstrate this clearly through that sister in order to give the others a firm confidence in everything that she had said. So that they might believe it more strongly, he wanted to show that what the holy mother had promised them was true.

33. Whatever the blows received or the trials that may come its way, there is no need to fear that this institution will perish, for it is in God's constant care. Nor does any member have anything to fear if

[32] Clare's Rule had been approved 22 years earlier, in 1253.

she is pure, and faithful to the order. God will defend us and will respond to all the questions that we may encounter, for he knows about the institution and is familiar with it and he loves it because of the worthiness of the holy mother and of the holy father, Friar Hugh, who gave us the doctrine and planted it firmly in us. There is no fear that God would let any sister perish who governed herself well under Saint Francis's direction.

34. In the year of the incarnation of Jesus Christ 1278, on the 17th day of the month of October, on a Sunday, the holy remains of the blessed father and holy brother, Hugh of Digne, and of the blessed mother, his sister, my lady Saint Douceline, were transferred to the new church of the Friars Minor of Marseilles. On that occasion, out of respect for God and Our Lady, a large number of the leaders of the order came together at the convent in Marseilles; and most of the sisters from the convent of Hyères came. There was a large gathering of devout people who came to take part in the joyous celebration to honour the holy remains.

35. All the orders of Marseilles and all the processions assembled. Then they lifted up the holy bodies and placed each of them in a rich sheet of gold. They were carried very reverently and with the utmost respect by the leaders of the order, ministers, guardians, lectors and other dignitaries of the highest rank. With great solemnity they carried them in a huge procession around the ramparts of Marseilles, joyfully singing the praises of God and Our Lady and my lord Saint Francis. All the people of Marseilles were there, both rich and poor. In their abundant faith, they crowded around the holy bodies in such a way that the processions could not enter the church because of the crush. All of them, both great and small, displayed a wonderful devotion to the holy remains.

36. They carried them into the friars' new church, with innumerable torches lit in their honour. Afterwards, a very solemn mass was celebrated; and then, honouring them with dignity and rejoicing, they placed them reverently in marble tombs in the choir of Notre-Dame, where they still remain, to the honour of the omnipotent God *qui es[t] benedictus in secula* [who is blessed forever].

Chapter Fifteen

Chapter fifteen is about the miracles that God accomplished through the Saint after her death.

1. Rejoice, then, daughters of Roubaud, both at Hyères and at Marseilles, for you had a most worthy person leading you when your order was founded. She served the Lord in complete sanctity. May He be always loved and served faithfully among you, through the gracious merits of the mother who established you, and by whose intercession God brought help to many people, as you are about to hear.

2. In Provence, there was a noble baron by the name of Raynaud, the lord of a castle called Cabriès. His wife was named Constance. They both very much wanted a son, but had been unable to have one. Confidently, they promised the Saint that if she wished to give them a son, they would offer her the child's weight in wax. Before long they had a fine son who brought them great happiness. He was so intelligent that people were amazed when he talked, and they felt that he was not like a child. The boy had such a fine mind that he appeared to be a special gift from God.

3. They also had another son who fell ill and was dying. They saw that he was in the throes of death and thought that the soul had left the body. At that, his mother was filled with the most profound grief and, turning in prayer to the Saint with bitter cries, she vowed without hesitation that she would visit her tomb, carrying the child with his shroud. When she had made this vow, the child was completely restored to life and good health.

4. That is how, through the merits of the blessed Saint, God in his mercy gave them back the child that they thought was dead, just as he had given them the first son through her intercession. So the mother joyfully kept her promise to her and told people that there was no doubt that the Saint had brought him back to life.

5. There was a woman in Marseilles who had lost all her children at birth. She was so despondent about this that she seemed to have lost her senses because of the grief that each of the children had caused her. Once, when she was nearing the end of a pregnancy, she was distraught, fearing that the child would die; she was grieving for him even before he was born.

6. One night as she slept, the blessed mother appeared to her, honourably accompanied by 12 more of the sisters of Roubaud who had already left this life; they all looked extremely beautiful. The Saint spoke very kindly to the woman and said, "I have come to tell you that you are carrying a son who will bring you joy, and you may be sure that great prosperity will come to you as a result of this, for I am telling you that he will live because I have asked to God to save him." Then the woman asked her who she was. "I am Douceline of Digne," the saint told her, "a beguine of Roubaud and sister of Brother Hugh of Digne. I left this world to go to God just this year. I am the one you called upon."

7. At this, the woman fell at her feet, earnestly asking her to bless her womb. So the Saint placed her hand on her and blessed her; then she disappeared. The woman remained comforted and had complete confidence in what the Saint had said to her. She hoped that through her merits she would find grace before God. And indeed the dream that the woman had came true; she gave birth to a son who made her very happy because he lived and became a successful merchant, giving her everything she could wish for and supporting her for many years.

8. A young noblewoman from the city of Marseilles, by the name of Cecilia, had suffered for a year from a serious eye ailment. She could barely tolerate any light; the white of her eye had become so red that it constantly looked as if her eye was bleeding. The doctors were unable to cure it with eye lotions or any other remedy.

9. As the blessed Saint's birthday was approaching, the day on which the community of Roubaud honours her memory, one of her sisters, named Carpenella, had been received into the order to become a daughter of the holy mother. She was supposed to enter Roubaud at that very time. This sister told her that she too should promise herself to the Saint; otherwise she was sure that she would not be cured.

10. So the young lady prayed devoutly to the Saint, and earnestly vowed that if she cured her on the day on which they honoured her memory, she would bring her as an offering a pound of wax in the shape of eyes, and that as long as she lived she would offer her a special candle on that day. As soon as she had made the promise, she felt an immediate improvement, and on the Saint's feast day, the day that she had requested, she was completely cured and never again had that trouble. She was faithful to her promise and kept her vow as long as she lived.

11.   In the town of Saint-Maximin there was a woman who was almost blind as a result of a terrible disease that made her eyes blood-red. It had reached the point that she could no longer see. She had been like this for many days, suffering great pain in her eyes.

12.   One night she was in great pain, sitting up in bed, unable to sleep at all. She was in complete despair, thinking that she would never be able to see again, and that she would be unable to find anyone who could tell her of a remedy. While she was having these thoughts, she remembered the Saint and began to pray fervently to her, weeping all the while. And suddenly she felt a hand pass over her eyes and immediately she saw clearly, and her pain went away.

13.   Then the woman was overcome with happiness and asked who it was who had cured her. And the answer came, "Douceline of Digne; go to her tomb." And she saw her in front of her, accompanied by three beguines. From that time on, the woman was completely devoted to her; and for a long time, whenever she come to Marseilles, she would first make a pilgrimage to her tomb. And she never suffered from that illness again.

14.   It so happened that a beguine of Roubaud, from the convent in Marseilles, was seriously ill and near death. She was given extreme unction and had lost the power of speech. She showed all the signs of someone about to die. As everyone watched, she was drifting away. Then one of the women there knelt down, weeping profusely, and she called on the Saint and made a vow in an attempt to save her. At that very moment, the one who had been sick began to speak and that night her illness ended, the fever left her, and she was cured.

15.   In the convent of Roubaud at Hyères, the lady Laura of Hyères was extremely ill with swelling in her neck and face; the doctors were giving up hope that she would recover. In this state, the sister who was ill asked in her heart for the blessed mother's help, and in her devotion she requested that she be given something from the Saint's relics. They brought her a finger of the holy virgin which she took very reverently. Guided by her strong faith and piety, she put it in her mouth where she felt the most pain, because she had every confidence that she would be healed with her help. And by doing this, the devout sister was restored to good health as she had asked, through the merits of the holy mother in whom she had put her hope and confidence. The swelling in her head, neck and face disappeared because the impure humours had been diverted, and she did not suffer the illness again.

16. The daughter of a rich man from Marseilles, named Barthélemy Martin, was gravely ill with a constant high fever. The little child, who was only a year old, had five abscesses on her body that would not break, and so her body was racked with pain. No one knew what to do about it; neither the doctors nor anyone else could carry out any procedure because the infant was so tender. All the doctors felt that she would die, and said that there was no natural way that she could escape it. And so the child became so seriously ill that she was near death. Everyone saw that her life was slipping away and felt sure that they would soon be burying her.

17. Her father and mother prayed devoutly to the Saint, asking for her help; they promised her that if she restored the child's life they would put her in Roubaud when she was old enough. What a wonderful thing God's goodness is! At the very moment they made their vow, the child improved, all her abscesses suddenly broke open, her fever went away and she was perfectly well.

18. On another occasion, when this same child, whom they called Alaiette Martin or Raouline, was about two years old, she became gravely ill. She was terribly swollen and her abdomen seemed ready to burst. She was extremely pale, and for more than five days she had not nursed at her mother's breast or taken any nourishment. She was clearly dying, and, in the opinion of those who were watching over her, death was about to take her.

19. The sisters of Roubaud sent her some water in which they had dipped one of the Saint's fingers which they kept in a silver reliquary. And as soon as her mother gave her the water to drink, the child began to get better. In three days the swelling had gone down, and the child they thought they were about to bury was completely healed.

20.   Some of this same water was given to a servant at Roubaud, whose name was Doucette. She had been suffering for almost two years from a serious stomach ailment that prevented her from digesting her food. It had reached the point that she could barely eat and could hardly keep anything down. She was so swollen that she could not bend over or put on her shoes. She was becoming emaciated from her illness and felt that she was going to die from it.

21.   No one could suggest anything to help her; any medicine she took or any advice that the doctors gave her only made her worse, and her strength was running out. But as soon as she drank with devotion from the water in which the holy mother's finger had been dipped, that very night she was completely cured. She recovered her appetite immediately and was able to take off her own shoes. She had been sick for more than a year, but from that time on she was free of the illness.

22.   Maragde Porcellet, a beguine of Roubaud, was the niece of my lady Philippine, who for many years was the head prioress and director of that holy institution. This young woman had a serious ailment that frequently took away her ability to speak. Among many other problems that she suffered from, she would get hiccups that were so strong they could be heard for some distance. No doctor had been able to cure her of them. But she drank, as the others had, some of the water in which they had bathed the Saint's finger, and as soon as she drank it, the girl was cured of the hiccups that had tormented her for such a long time. It was because of the Saint's virtue that they left her.

23.   Another time, that same young woman had lost the ability to speak because her disorder had caused her tongue to go so far back into her throat that no one could see it or touch it. She had been unable to speak for three days. As the day was approaching on which the sisters held their annual celebration in honour of the Saint, all the women were saddened, out of the compassion that they had for her. So they prayed humbly and devoutly to the holy mother, asking her to take pity on the girl and grant her the favour of being able to honour her on that day and of having God restore her tongue so that she could recover her speech.

24.   When Saturday evening came, she still could not speak, so in silence she carried out some acts of piety to honour the Saint. The others told her to have faith in her because they were sure that she would cure her. She gestured to them and showed them with signs that she had every confidence that she would recover her speech on the Saint's day. Nevertheless one of them, who was becoming impatient, said, "Truly, glorious mother, I will not be satisfied if she has not spoken tomorrow, before the mealtime reading, so that we can hear your life read with greater joy." It was to be read for the first time in the convent that day.

25. The next night, Maragde was still unable to talk. As she slept, she heard in her sleep a voice speaking to her very gently and compassionately. It was saying, "You should know, Maragde, that because of the wonderful prayers that have been said for you, God is restoring your speech. When you waken, you will find that you can speak, and you will continue to be able to talk until the upcoming feast day of Our Lady." Now this celebration was eight days away.

26. "But I am also telling you", she said tenderly, "that by the time five days have passed after the feast of the mother of God, you will have lost it again; so you will be discouraged when you recover it. People will pray to a great number of saints and call on them for help, but you must understand that you will not recover your speech through anyone's efforts until God decides to give it to you. You will be mute for such a long time that people will lose all hope that you will ever speak again, but in the end you will be able to."

27. Maragde did not see the person who was speaking to her; she only heard the words. But she knew at once in her heart that the one who was speaking to her was the holy mother, to whom she had been praying that night in her heart and to whom the sisters had been devoutly praying on her behalf, asking that she regain her speech that day. Then she woke up and found that her tongue was long enough for her to speak a little. First she made the sign of the cross, then she called for my lady Philippine who was her mother and the mother of all of the others. Then she got up and came to the others and joyfully told them how the holy mother had restored her speech to her.

28. And just as she had been told in her dream, she spoke for the period of time that the Saint had specified. Then, on the fifth day after the feast of Our Lady, again as she had been told, she lost the ability to speak and did not recover it for more than six weeks, no matter what saints were invoked, until it pleased God to restore it to her.

29.   Many other people were healed in the same way: when they drank some of the water in which the holy mother's finger had been dipped, they were immediately cured of the infirmities from which they suffered.

30.   There was a man in Marseilles who was leading such a sinful life that, to judge by his misdeeds, he seemed to be out of his mind. His father and mother were deeply troubled by this, as were all his friends, for he was disobeying God and everyone else. He was no longer himself and did not know what he was doing; nor would he listen to anyone, for he was completely depraved. He had been living this wicked life for a long time. During this period, when his friends were worrying about him, they were devoutly given some of the Saint's relics. His distressed parents took them and confidently placed them in the clothes that he was wearing, in such a way that he was unaware of it.

31.   As soon as he had the relics on his person, he quickly became himself again, through God's power. He returned to God with a heavy heart for the evil things he had done, and made amends for his wrongs. He turned his life around and from then on lived blamelessly, never returning to his old ways. He obeyed his parents, accomplished good deeds, and died honourably.

32.   Through the merits of the Saint, God granted many people the opportunity to change their life and turn away from sin, when they sincerely made their appeal to her. It has been recognized in various situations that the Saint is a special source of help for troubled souls when they call upon her in their distress. It is clear that she brings comfort and help in times of spiritual affliction, when people turn to her.

33.   There was a man who was devoted to the Saint and often came to the church to visit her tomb. One night he was taken seriously ill and all night long the people where he lived thought he was dying. He seemed to be out of his mind, rolling around on the floor through the whole house. No one could restrain him, and he wanted to throw himself down the stairs. He was not talking, but he was uttering such terrible groans that they thought he was going to die. This agony went on almost all night, and no one could determine what the illness was, but it appeared that he had gone mad.

34. When this had gone on for a long while, to the point that his wife and the others were completely dismayed and astounded, he gave a loud shout, crying out, "Help me, Saint Douceline." He later said that while he was unable to talk, he had been calling to her in his heart. But as soon as he said her name, he found his cure and was healed. He spit out all the poison or humour that was causing his suffering, and was entirely free of his affliction, completely cured and healthy. Not wanting to be ungrateful for the blessing he had received, the good man made his way to the Saint's tomb with a candle the very morning that he was cured of his illness.

35. When he was still a child, Brother Pellegrin Reppellin was cured by the Saint of a paralysis that he had had from birth in all his limbs. As soon as the crippled limbs were healed and straightened by the power of God, the holy woman had his mother promise that he would become a Friar Minor and son of Saint Francis. And when he reached the proper age, he was in fact received into the order. He went on to become a preacher, he was a confessor for a long period of time, and for a while he was the precentor at the convent in Marseilles.

36. While he was in that convent, he told of the many miracles and blessings that he had received from God through the merits of the Saint after she died. He said that at the time when he was about to enter the order, he had a secular brother who objected strongly to his becoming a Friar Minor, and wanted him to become a monk instead. This is how it happened.

37. One day, his brother was taking him to the monastery of Saint Victor to have him accepted there. He was going only because he had been forced to and because he was afraid of the brother. Suddenly he felt a terrible pain in one of his ears that had earlier been cured through the Saint's virtue. The further he went and the closer he came to the monastery, the worse the pain became. When he was inside the church and they were about to put the robes on him, his ear, neck and throat became so swollen that he could barely speak, and he had to return home.

38.   When he reached home, he could not speak until he remembered the vow that the Saint had had him make. Then he turned to her in his heart, promising and vowing that if she cured him and restored his ability to speak, he would do everything in his power to fulfill his promise to enter the Order of Saint Francis. As soon as he had formed this resolve in his heart, the swelling in his neck and ear went down, his throat was clear, and he began to speak.

39.   It was obvious to everyone that the Saint was insisting that he keep the vow that she had wanted him to make, for twice he had to be taken away from the monastery in the same way. Each time his neck swelled up, as has been described. For their part, the friars did not want to accept him, but when they saw the miracle the second time, they could not dispute it. So out of respect for the Saint and for the promise, they admitted him into the order and he was made a Friar Minor.

40.   The Saint did many other miracles that through negligence were not fully investigated. Through her merits, God rescued many people in their time of need and still saves them when they call on her with all their heart.

41.   Blessed be God forever, who has seen that this story of her life has been brought to completion. In it have been shown the virtue and merits of the Saint and the goodness of God. And if this has been done well, it should not be attributed to the knowledge or understanding of the person writing, for she has written about and set forth many things that, through her own lack of understanding, she does not comprehend. The person responsible for it is crude and coarse and uneducated. But the master of all truth, who knows everything and who has more knowledge of the extent of the Saint's merits than does any human, this Lord has been the principal author and master of this work.

42.   That is why whatever has been done well should be attributed only to God; and the serious faults that may be found in it are due only to this person's ignorance and ineptitude. She protests strongly and sincerely that she has set out nothing in this that has come from her own imagination; everything is in accordance with the truth and entirely as the people who experienced it faithfully and truthfully described it.

43.   The miracles that are recounted here are beyond doubt, for not one was written down that was not proved and that was not learned from the people to whom it happened or from the most trustworthy witnesses who attested that they saw it with their own eyes and heard it. To dispel any doubts or suspicion, we swear that what we have put in writing is told truthfully. We have left out many other miracles that we learned about from the people involved but did not write down because we did not have reliable or sworn testimony.

HERE END THE SAINT'S MIRACLES FOR WHICH GOD BE PRAISED NOW AND FOREVER. AMEN.

Chapter Sixteen

1.   Let the daughters of such a respected mother, so deserving of emulation, be joyful. May they rejoice in Our Lord who has called them into her holy order, to follow in her footsteps and aspire to her perfection. May they strive to be like their mother.

2.   May they remember the one who has led them; surely in our time there has never been a better woman or one more accomplished in every virtue. In her, every perfection was fulfilled, for she engaged in no virtue without carrying it to the highest degree.

3.   She was filled with spiritual wisdom and yet was poor in spirit; she was superior in God's blessings, but superior also in humility.

4.   She was patient in the face of adversity and scorn, and endured these things graciously. She rejoiced in her tribulations and afflictions and accepted them with great delight.

5.   She did not place her hopes in false riches, but in holy poverty, and so she had everything in abundance. She did not give her heart to the false delights of the world, but to the heavenly kingdom.

6.   She fled from temporal pleasures and abhorred all honours and earthly pride.

7.   She followed reason and loved truth, standing firm and strong against all the assaults of sin.

8.   She was terrible in her reprimands and chastisements, and just in her discipline, punishing with severity and authority.

9.   She was always ready to forgive, and full of mercy where there was humble repentance.

10.   She was as mild, gracious and gentle in her administration as she was in giving comfort, treating everyone with the same kindness, with a wonderful equanimity.

11.   She respected the elderly and her superiors. In the spirit of God's charity, she loved her neighbour as herself.

12.   She suffered with those who suffered, and was quick to help them in their suffering. She grieved with the wretched and the afflicted.

13.   She cared for the poor and served the sick, making it her habit to visit them with extraordinary compassion.

14.   She helped in all these ways for God's sake, and would be very distressed when she could not find a way to do what she so much wanted.

15.   She was faithful in prayer, and there was warmth in her devotion.

16.   She was passionate in her love of God and fervent in her contemplation.

17.   Entirely prepared to suffer martyrdom, she showed her desire for it.

18.   She was diligent in everything she did, especially in reading and praying. She was particularly attentive to saying her hours.

19.   She was extremely gracious in her charity, pure in her innocence, and honest in everything.

20.   She was full of goodness and accomplished in virtue.

21.   She was exceedingly constant and resolute, and was not easily swayed. For once she put her hand to the plough in God's service, she never looked back, aspiring to perfection in her thinking, in her deeds and in her desires. That is why she possessed the beauty of the purest chastity and the nobleness of virginity, which produce white blossoms, a sweet fragrance to God.

22. She can say with honesty that she scorned the world and all its adornments for the love of Christ whom she now sees face to face, in whom she believed, and whom she has always loved completely and sought after with all her strength. And so she will rejoice endlessly in paradise with God, whom she has loved and desired.

23. Oh what an amazing woman! Surrounded by the mists of this world, she shone like the morning star that is called Lucifer! By shining in the new ways she found of practising virtue, she chased away all the shadows of error. The rays of her goodness spread throughout Provence, and even beyond Provence, lighting the way for many who were drawn to her institution by her love and her example.

24. At the beginning of her life she could truly declare: *"Ego sicut oliva fructifera in domo Dei.* Like the olive tree, I will produce abundant fruit in God's house."[33]

25. As her life blossomed, she could happily add: *"Ego mater pulcre dilectionis, mater supra modum mirabilis, et bonorum memoria digna.* I am the mother of a beautiful love, a mother who is outstanding because of the perfect things she has done, a mother who deserves to be remembered with blessings."[34]

26. At the peak of her virtue she could truly claim: *"Ego sicut vitis fructificavi suavitatem odoris, et flores mei fructus honoris et honestatis.* Like a fruitful vine, I have sent out a sweet fragrance and have borne flowers that produced good and honourable fruit."[35]

27. Joy to Hyères, for that is where she began her work in such a saintly way and where she carried it out so perfectly.

28. Joy to the town of Aix, where she developed her virtues with kindness and devotion.

---

33 Psalm 52:8.
34 This is the refrain of the Office of St. Douceline according to Gout, 274.
35 Ecclesiasticus (Apocrypha), 24:17.

29.   Joy to the noble city of Marseilles, where her life was so gloriously made complete.

30.   Joy, salvation and peace to the county of Provence, for you have been illuminated by her goodness.

31.   Joy to all those who took the holy name of beguine because she showed them the way of salvation through holy penitence.

32.   Joy, blessing and the peace of God to all the true, humble and beloved daughters of the holy mother; through her they learned the way of humility, charity, purity and perfection.

33.   Peace, strength and stability to the houses of Roubaud in Hyères and in Marseilles, for they received blessing, assurance and grace from the holy mother; the glory of God and eternal blessing are granted to all those sisters who will carry on faithfully and lovingly.

Prestante domino nostro Ihesu Cristo qui cum Deo Patre et Spiritu Sancto vivis et regnas, Deus benedictus, in secula seculorum. Amen.

[Through the goodness of Our Lord Jesus Christ who lives and reigns with God the Father and the Holy Spirit, blessed God, forever and ever. Amen.]

Obsecro vos qui hoc legeritis, ut Jacobi peccatoris in orationibus vestris memineritis. Amen

[You who read this, please remember the sinner Jacques[36] in your prayers. Amen.[37]]

---

[36]   We have no further information about the scribe of this manuscript.

[37]   The verso of the manuscript's final leaf (fol. 103v) contains the profession of faith and hymn of the beguines. The profession of faith of the beguines of Marseilles is as follows: I – whose name is – vow, pledge and donate my virginity with all my heart to God, my lady the Holy Virgin Mary, to our saintly father and our saintly mother, to all the saints of the heavenly court, keeping and preserving it until the end of my life without ever doing anything to put it in peril. I pray you my lady, and all of you, to be my guarantors before God on the Day of Judgement. At the same time, I vow and pledge obedience to Our Lord and Our Lady, to our saintly father and our saintly mother, to all the saints, [and] that I shall be steadfastly and solely obedient to you, my lady, and to all the prioresses who will follow you, preserving and maintaining the community of Roubaud in Marseilles as Pope John [XXII] confirmed it (Albanés, Pièces Justificatives, 257).

Interpretive Essay

Douceline de Digne: The "Douce et Digne" Mother of Roubaud

"Douce et Digne": this is how her biographer Philippine plays with Douceline's name and attempts to capture the essence of her personality (1:3). If there can be no doubts about her dignity, stature and the exceptional nature of her spiritual achievements, as the mother and guide of the Ladies of Roubaud, as source of inspiration for ecclesiastical or political leaders and an object of devotion for the humble people of Provence, her "sweetness" is more questionable. Reading her Life, we are more often confronted by examples of her rigour, applied to herself and required from her sisters, rigour manifested by the privations she imposed upon her body and the tortures she suffered as the price of recognition of her ecstasies and levitations. For the modern reader there seems to be more violence than sweetness in Douceline's journey. However, such a conclusion, based upon an apparent incompatibility, neglects the medieval sense of "coencidentia oppositorum", especially as it relates to the mystical experience. As we will see in this essay, the notion of paradox comes easily to mind when we attempt to account for the profound ambivalence of mysticism and try to resolve what we tend to see as contradictions. Through rigour and asceticism, the mystics reach the peculiar form of sweetness they are yearning for, a joy which transcends suffering. This was particularly true for Douceline de Digne whose inspiration was the sweet St. Francis.

Another fundamental opposition which is deconstructed by the experience of women mystics, most strikingly so in Douceline's case, is the dichotomic division between the soul and the body, where the flesh, seen an obstacle to spiritual progress, must be repressed. In fact, what we see in their Lives, is the overwhelming presence of the body as the vehicle and privileged channel of God, the inescapable manifestation of His presence. Extreme asceticism results in the extreme paradox: complete forgetfulness of the body coexisting with a constant preoccupation with bodily needs, with the flesh and its fluids, a state rewarded by very concrete marks of validation, the most spectacular being the stigmata and levitation. Corresponding to the mortified and tortured body is the ecstatic, raptured body, channelling the word of God and invested with the ability to cure other bodies, the ability to perform miracles being incontestable proof of having reached the status of sainthood. The debased and tormented body of the human sinner is, as result of this sign of election, sanctified as a relic. This process of mystical inversion is particularly explicit in Douceline's Life, and becomes one of its central threads, through Philippine's lengthy descriptions of crowds flocking around the saint's levitating body and wanting to touch it. The publicity of the phenomenon and its theatricalization are a constitutive part of the scenario in their apparent contradiction with Douceline's vow of humility: they are for her a source of pain and suffering which, in turn, contribute to the joy she is yearning for.

In the essay which follows we intend to examine the Life of Douceline de Digne in relation to the oppositions, which are at the core of this text. Commencing with the paradoxes of asceticism and mortification which marked her road to sanctity, we will then explore her visions and miracle-working powers, as they are described by her biographer. We will demonstrate that the welfare and continuity of her order was a central, all-encompassing concern for Douceline, and we will next examine the way in which she shaped her order and the nature of the theology which inspired that work, concluding our discussion with an analysis of Douceline's identification with the Holy Virgin and a discussion of the "voice" of the vita's author, Philippine Porcellet.

Asceticism and Mortification: the Road to Sanctity

The life of Douceline, like the "hagiobiographies" of the Belgian beguines, follows the pattern, which can be clearly identified in the thirteenth century, as one of conversion and spiritual journey, culminating in sainthood.[1] In order to evaluate Douceline's uniqueness, we should first sketch the lines of the standard mystic life as it emerges from their biographies.[2] They normally begin with a brief presenta-

---

[1] Greenspan 218. See note 109 in the Introduction above.

[2] In his study of sacred biography, Heffernan states that each Life places the concept of the individual within the larger frame of exemplary types illustrating the timeless reality of the sacred (87–88). The genre develops according to narrative and rhetorical conventions mostly borrowed from the *Passio Sanctae Perpetuae et Felicitatis* (192): virginity, espousal to Christ, visions, gift of the spirit and martyrdom (234). See also Vauchez 1981, 247–48 and 1991, 31.

earthly love and family life for a total union with Christ is a frequent motive for refusing marriage and making the vow of chastity.[9] As Lutgard of Aywières said to a suitor in rejecting him: "I have been overtaken by another lover", bridal love for the Beloved being "one of the salient characteristics of beguine mysticism".[10] However, there is nothing as graphic in Douceline's attachment to Christ as the descriptions we find in the lives of the pious Belgian women (3:7; 7:7; 9:49; 9:56).[11]

An interpretation of this mystic eroticism in terms of female masochism totally bypasses the cultural and theological meaning of suffering, a level of meaning that must be also be applied to the other forms of bodily manipulations. Fasting, deprivation of sleep, and self-inflicted wounds were ways of mortifying the body that were an almost compulsory feature of the saintly life, often manifest since

9 Vauchez 1987a, 195, 198; Heffernan, 188–89; Newman 1995, 31–32. For a definition of chastity through penitential practices applying to a mixed audience, not only virgins, see Muessig 1996. Newman (1998, 742), in a memorable phrase, refers to "the currency of love's exchange".

10 Lutgard of Aywières (Thomas de Cantimpré 1991, 24 and 31) where she exchanges her heart with Jesus; see also Margaret of Ypres (Thomas de Cantimpré 1996, 20–22); Yvette of Huy (Hugh of Floreffe, 47); Birgitta (Gregersson and Gascoigne, 24). The terms of lover, spouse, bridegroom, referring to the divine object of love, must be taken in their full implications, which include an erotic yearning for a total fusion with Christ. Examples of the mystic's yearning for a total union with Christ can be found in Margaret of Ypres (39, 46) and Lutgard of Aywières (36–37). For "bridal mysticism" see Roisin (1947, 109–12), Newman, 1995 (143), and Wiethaus (1991, 42–49) for German and Flemish beguines.

11 Lutgard of Aywières leaned on the couch of the Bridegroom (Thomas de Cantimpré 1991, 85), Yvette of Huy was caught up in the caresses and kisses of the Beloved whenever she prayed (Hugh of Floreffe, 109); Marie d'Oignies would feel as if her head was lying upon the knees of Christ (Jacques de Vitry, 133) or would hold him tightly between her breasts like a baby and kiss him as if he were an infant. Even if we can recognize, in this last image, devotion to the child Christ, so well represented by Margaret Ebner (Schmidt and Hindsley 53–59), this does not obliterate the sensual impression conveyed by the scene. See also the very graphic scene with Lutgard of Aywières: "Christ in the appearance of a lamb positioned himself on her breast in such a manner that one foot was on her right shoulder and the other on the left. He placed His mouth on her mouth, and by sucking would draw out from her breast a melody" (38). In many cases, however, the sweetness of rapture in Christ's love is accompanied by the pain of sharing his sacrifice. Marie d'Oignies was "tortured in body with the love for Christ and delight" (62), a sweetness described in Lutgard's Life as a physical embrace initiated by Christ who pressed "the mouth of her heart" against "the bloody wound in His side" (34–34). Examples of erotic imagery in Bell 109; Bynum 1982, 178, 257, and 1987, 162; Wiethaus 1991, 42–45.

childhood as a sign of election. They cannot be understood either as a simple rejection of the body along the lines of the dichotomy between the purified soul and the flesh as the locus of evil, women being to men as the body is to the soul.[12] Such a division, especially during the thirteenth century, might come close to heresy and be confused with the Cathar dualism, the radical opposition of the principles of Good and Evil. Rather, the group of northern beguines under the Cistercian and Dominican influence, as well as Douceline with her active Franciscanism, were themselves part of a campaign against heresy targeting lay religiosity.[13] The result is the paradox of constant pressures from spiritual advisors teaching the value of moderation and the virtue of discretion in practising asceticism, and the fierce determination of the women mystics to prove themselves as "athletes" of mortification.[14] That could provoke an open conflict, as when Yvette of Huy disobeyed the religious men who advised her to temper her rigour, an attitude that led her biographer to comment that when she finally agreed to observe temperance, she served God more religiously and more wisely.[15] Jacques de Vitry reminds the reader that the excesses of Marie d'Oignies's fervour are a privilege for a few and must be admired rather than imitated.[16] Thomas de Cantimpré cites Augustine's authority in the *City of God* for his plea in favour of moderation, and uses Lutgard of Aywières's example for

---

[12] For a critique of too rigid a dichotomy in associating woman with the body and man with the soul, see Boureau, Murk-Jansen (1996 in Chance, 53), and McNamara (in Wiethaus 1993) for the anti-Cathar concept of the union of the flesh and spirit. We share Beckwith's positive interpretation of self-mortification as a form of valorization, a way to achieve redemption through physicality (206). See also Wiethaus (1991) for a positive, non masochistic view of suffering and a nuanced interpretation of the relationship between soul and body in female mysticism, refining Bynum's (1986) definition of the female denoted as a genderless self in women writers; and Kay and Rubin (5) on the troubling proximity of these incommensurable yet coexisting entities.

[13] Bolton 1978, 253.

[14] About the prescription of moderation in self-mortification in the Old Testament and the Fathers, see Bell, 118–19.

[15] Yvette of Huy (Hugh of Floreffe, 73–75). Moderation is usually a matter of negotiation between the woman and the spiritual advisor, he urging her to sleep or to talk See, for example, Margaret of Ypres (Thomas de Cantimpré 1996, 28, 34). For other examples see Margaret of Cortona, ordered to eat because she was committing suicide with her fasting (Bell, 102) and Clare of Assisi, ordered to eat by St. Francis (Bell, 124).

[16] Jacques de Vitry, 54–55.

the instruction of those who reject their bodies.[17] He praises her discretion and the fact that she did not want to weaken her body by extreme fasting.[18] Douceline's teaching to her spiritual daughters also warned them against excessive austerity and recommended a middle path (5:11; 6:12). This middle path, however, did not apply to Douceline herself. Rather, her attitude corresponded to Bynum's observation, that the extremism of religious women was more a reaction against the theologians and preachers' advocacy of moderation than an internalization of their views on the body and femininity.[19] Already when she lived in her father's house, along with her dedication to humility, she wanted to reach the highest levels of spirituality, her model being Saint Cecilia. Like her, she used to wear a hair shirt under her fine clothing and bound herself with a knotted cord "and at the place where the knots dug into her flesh there were often worms" (1:10–11). She used to sleep only one-third of the night, on a bed made with straw, praying and reading the first third and doing her matins during the last, "and so that sleep would bring her no rest, she would attach a rope above her bed, and she would tie the other end of the rope around herself so that as soon as she moved, the rope would pull on her and she would wake up" (1:12). However, even after her conversion and dedication to the life of a beguine, there is no special emphasis on her fasting, which is presented simply as a consequence of her attraction to God; she often forgot to eat and fell into ecstasy. In fact, even if she observed abstinence and could spend a day without eating or drinking as a form of sacrifice, food is seen as positive, a channel for orison and rapture, the earthly table being for her a reminder of the communion table (9:2). Her severe self-mutilations were inflicted, not as a form of punishment or purification, but on the contrary, were the result of her efforts to maintain her body in its normal functions. She tried, for example, to escape her ecstasies and raptures by means of the pain caused by needles stuck into her hands (9:31–34).

By comparison, most practices of the Belgian devout women were more systematically self-mutilating. To the usual wearing of the hair shirt or knotted cord, there was the frequent addition of beating with

---

[17] Thomas de Cantimpré 1991, 62–63.
[18] Christ intervenes also to ask Margaret of Ypres to restrain her weeping (Thomas de Cantimpré 1996, 34) and Margaret of Cortona to reduce her abstinence (Bell, 100).
[19] Bynum 1987, 238; Vauchez 1987a, 194.

chains, iron nails or thorns, burning the skin with drops of a wax candle or even cutting off large pieces of one's own flesh with a knife.[20] More revealing than the ways they tortured themselves are the reasons that are provided for inflicting such sufferings to their bodies. The will to subdue the body and weaken it in order to purify and free the soul is not the most frequently mentioned intention.[21] For Douceline, corporal mortifications were primarily a form of communication with God, of prayer. Upon learning that the Saracens had captured the nuns of Antioch, she asked the sisters of both houses, in Hyères and Marseilles, to "practice discipline, to fast, to weep and to cry to God with bitter tears for mercy" (7:4). Proof that her admonitions had been completely integrated by her followers is provided by their precise observance of this behaviour at her death: they practiced flagellation, fasted with bread and water, kneeling on the ground (13:11). The body becomes a message, a message to God which has to be expressed through its coded manifestations.

Love is the most frequently mentioned motivation for bodily mortification in the vitae: love for the Crucified Christ, in sharing his sacrifice, and for fellow humans in suffering to redeem their souls from Purgatory.[22] Douceline insists on charity, a *compassion de caritat* which finds its justification in Christ's Passion. This justification explains how her real compassion for the affliction of the suffering finds its limits; rather than providing support, Douceline rebukes a widow who lamenting the loss of her husband, a mere

---

20 Wearing of hair shirt or knotted cord: Yvette of Huy (Hugh of Floreffe, 36), Marie d'Oignies (Jacques de Vitry, 54, 78), Birgitta (Gregersson and Gascoigne, 21); beating: Marie d'Oignies (69), Margaret of Ypres (Thomas de Cantimpré 1996, 31); with chains or iron nails: Dauphine of Puimichel (Cambell, 183), Yvette of Huy (Hugh of Floreffe, 36); with thorns: Christina the Astonishing (Thomas de Cantimpré 1999b, 23), Margaret of Ypres (Thomas de Cantimpré 1996, 10, 19); burning oneself: Birgitta (Gregersson and Gascoigne, 22); cutting oneself, Marie d'Oignies (Jacques de Vitry, 63, 79). See Tibbetts Schulenberg on the tradition of the "heroics of virginity".

21 Mentioned also in the vitae of Marie d'Oignies (Jacques de Vitry, 117) and Christina the Astonishing (Thomas de Cantimpré 1999b, 42).

22 We concur with Bynum's remark (1991, 54) that for many thirteenth- and fourteenth-century pious women, "suffering was acting and vice versa", especially in the context of the beguines' christocentrism (McDonnell 151). See her chapter on "The Female Body and Religious Practice in the Later Middle Ages" (1991, 181–238), Constable and Vauchez (1981, 224–25, 451) for male counterparts. For a consideration of the place given to Purgatory by the Belgian beguines, an element missing from Le Goff's study, see Sweetman 616–22 and McNamara 1991 in Blumenfeld-Kosinski and Szell, 212–18.

mortal man, while the Saviour has been lost through sin (7:7). The spectacular performances of Christina the Astonishing and her whole spiritual journey, find their *raison d'être* in the mission of redeeming souls. Creeping into ovens, throwing herself into roaring fires, jumping into cauldrons of boiling water, stretching her arms and legs on the rack on which brigands were tormented, suspending herself on the gallows between the thieves, provoking dogs and running through woods thick with thorns[23] were Christina's ways of performing her duty of suffering for the sins of men. Her attitude is not primarily one of detestation and rejection of her body. In a very touching scene, we see her weeping over her feet, then smiling and taking them with both hands, kissing their soles "with greatest affection" because she had tormented her "most beloved body".[24] Her biographer, Thomas Cantimpré, in reporting these odd examples of mortification, provides the proper interpretative framework, explaining them as the form of apostolate she had been mandated to perform.[25]

Weeping was often practised as a form of mortification. Not a sentimental, involuntary response, it was a rigorous aspect of devotional behaviour. A manifestation of beguines' sorrow for Christ's Passion, Douceline recommended it to her daughters as the sign of their vocation: "a beguine was made for weeping, and not for singing" (3:8). The sorrow shown on their faces she considered just as important for identifying them as the mantles covering their heads. According to her vita, she "washed herself, day and night, in a great shower of tears", after midnight until matins, and at the appointed hours, even when she was sick (6:13–14). Her continual weeping provoked serious headaches that recall the eye-trouble St. Francis developed for the same reason (6:15; 9:4).[26] Dauphine combined head and eye disorders and answered to her confessor that she would prefer being blind and losing her mind to abstaining from tears, by which the spirit is purified and refined.[27] It seems indeed that in order to be effective the grace of tears had to manifest itself in the most extreme form. Marie d'Oignies wept showers of tears which disturbed the priest during the mass. The ground in the church became muddy, the book and the altar cloths were dripping and she

---

[23] Christina the Astonishing (Thomas de Cantimpré 1999b, 21–23).
[24] *Ibid.*, 43.
[25] *Ibid.*, 19. On intercession as the mandate of beguines, Newman 1995, 109–13; on the hagiographer as an interpreter of the mystic's experience, Simons, 19.
[26] Habig, 668. Vauchez (1981, 512–13) for the gift of tears as a mark of holiness.
[27] Cambell 202–203: a nun squeezed out Dauphine's veil and collected her tears in a vial.

had often to change her veil for a dry one.[28] The reasons given for
these manifestations of excessive sorrow echo those concerning
other practices of mortification including, as we will see, fasting.
They express the women's compassion for Christ's suffering and
their empathy for the souls of sinners, including their own.[29]

Fasting also serves the same purpose of purifying the body and
preparing for the mystical union with God and it is a justification
invoked by Douceline herself for requiring a "moderate abstinence"
which would "maintain purity of body and soul, in herself and in the
others" (6:3).[30] Self-abasement and self-abandonment in favour of a
complete identification with God through his incarnation "is not
symptom, it is theology"[31] in the vitae of the mystics. This explains
the recurrent practice, often associated with fasting, of eating vile
and loathsome food, adding to them something unpleasant like
cinders or wild plants.[32] But fasting may also be seen as a positive
way to identify with the struggle of the Church against heretics or as
an act which assists in the salvation of souls.[33] Representing fasting,
like weeping, as a kind of prayer is closer to Douceline's attitude than
the more extreme forms of food rejection, evident when Marie
d'Oignies, revolted by the smell of bread, began to cry out, spit, and
gasp with anxiety.[34] Food, for Douceline, was an occasion to
abandon herself to contemplation: the table set and prepared
reminded her the sacrificial meal of the Holy Lamb. She simply

28 Marie d'Oignies (Jacques de Vitry, 58–60). See also *The Book of Margery Kempe* and Mahoney.
29 Examples in Margaret of Ypres (Thomas de Cantimpré 1996, 19), Marie d'Oignies (Jacques de Vitry, 58). Birgitta (Gregersson and Gascoigne, 15) wept for Christ's sacrifice. Tears for the sinners' sins in Christina the Astonishing (Thomas de Cantimpré 1999b, 30), Lutgard of Aywières (Thomas de Cantimpré 1991, 82, 85) Margaret of Ypres (Thomas de Cantimpré 1996, 25), Yvette of Huy (Hugh of Floreffe, 70, 72), Marie d'Oignies (Jacques de Vitry, 112), Birgitta (Gregersson and Gascoigne, 17), Dauphine (Cambell, 203).
30 As amply demonstrated by Bell in his study of "holy anorexia" and Bynum when she rightly relates fasting and feasting on the Eucharist (Bynum 1987, 200 sq.; Bynum 1991, 43–45, and concerning specifically the Flemish beguines, 119–50).
31 Bynum 1987, 206.
32 Eating vile food: Christina the Astonishing (Thomas de Cantimpré 1999b, 30); adding unpleasant things: Yvette of Huy (Hugh of Florette, 36) or wild plants: Marie d'Oignies (Thomas de Cantimpré 1991, 88). See also Bynum 1987, 165, 171.
33 For example in Lutgard of Aywières (Thomas de Cantimpré 1991, 45, 48, 52, 90) or Marie d'Oignies (Jacques de Vitry, 73).
34 Lutgard of Aywières was unable to swallow food (Thomas de Cantimpré 1991, 45).

forgot to eat, her rapture triggered by the nature of what was presented on the table, veal, for example, evoking the sacrificial calf (9:52–54). In many respects, the vow of poverty can be compared to fasting. In giving up their wealth, the women embraced another form of renunciation of worldly ties and pleasures. While Douceline espoused the strictest renunciation for herself, she and her brother preached moderation in this aspect to her ladies. However, material renunciation, like food deprivation, found its real meaning when combined with charity.[35] Like eating, resting and being idle were also forms of bodily indulgence which had to be cured by service and good work (6:8). Feeding and clothing the poor, tending the sick and assisting the dying were all ways of expressing an active compassion for the destitute of society while sharing their destiny. The question of poverty, as we will see, was not without socio-political implications, especially within the Franciscan context in which Douceline was moving.[36]

An aspect of ascetic behaviour that Douceline particularly favoured was deprivation of sleep. We have already described the installation she cleverly devised when she was still in her father's house in order to awaken her.[37] Not yet involved in the life of a religious woman, she sets rules for herself, dividing the night into three parts in a sort of quasi-liturgical organization of time: reading and prayer, rest and matins followed by prayers (1:8). The usual details described in the beguines' vitae mention beds made with straw or planks or without mattresses.[38] Marie d'Oignies, excessive in this ascetic behaviour as in others, did not even go to bed, but used to sit in the church, leaning her head against the wall, her heart awake even while when she slept, dreaming only of Christ.[39] Rather than an occa-

---

[35] Bynum's link between fasting and feeding the poor (1987, 245–78) is rather too restrictive.

[36] The division between men giving up money and women giving up food is not as clear-cut as Bynum suggests (Vauchez 1981, 234–40; Bynum 1987, 193). For more contextualized interpretations, see Rosenwein and Little, 16–32; Mollat, 119–90; McNamara 1991 in Blumenfeld-Kosinski and Szell; Little about the beguines (128–34), and the Franciscan and Dominican attitude toward poverty (146). For the Franciscans, see also Lambert and Burr 1989b.

[37] See above, 121.

[38] Beds made with straw: Dauphine de Puimichel (Cambell, 183); planks: Marie d'Oignies (Jacques de Vitry, 54); without mattress: Yvette of Huy (Hugh of Florette, 36).

[39] Marie d'Oignies (Jacques de Vitry, 76). She scorns those who enjoy soft beds (78).

sional ascetic behaviour, sleeplessness is an integral part of the pattern we are describing, a pattern – along with food deprivation, bodily mortification and the prohibition of sexuality – to which also belongs respect for silence and the control of speech.[40] Margaret of Ypres's discomfort with ordinary talk is a good illustration of the mystic's inability to maintain a normal life in the context of her choice of a world of meditation and prayers. Because she tended to limit her conversations to those she had with her spiritual father, he ordered her to talk with her mother and sisters as long as it would take to recite seven psalms.[41] She would fall asleep when compelled to hear "anything useless" or of "common currency in the world".[42] Douceline's role as spiritual advisor for the beguines of her community led her to legislate their speech; she used to teach them that excessive talking was a sin and anyone who indulged in talking about the world's vanities would be harshly chastized (6:9). Disapproving of idle words, she condemned telling lies to such extent that she would have sacrificed any liar with her own hands (6:10).

The escape from worldly preoccupations into the "desert" – albeit an interior one – or any form of solitary place, answers to the same urge. Anchoritic seclusion was a solution open to lay women who, like Yvette of Huy, found it difficult "to live among the worldly and not be worldly".[43] Their family's lack of understanding of their need for isolation resulted in constant tension between Margaret of Ypres and her mother and sisters in the house which the family shared, and also her sisters' efforts to prevent Christina the Astonishing's frequent flights to forests, tree tops, or to the tops of castles or churches.[44] Douceline's decision not to join an institutionalized order and to remain – with her companions – a lay religious woman, meant that she refused to be totally removed from the world; her first house was established in the countryside but close to the town of Hyères, and her second settlement was located in the same kind of space: the suburbs of Marseilles, outside the walls of the town. This pattern of

---

[40] Dauphine of Puimichel (Cambell, 44); Yvette of Huy (Hugh of Floreffe, 36); Marie d'Oignies (Jacques de Vitry, 65, 80). On the association between the vices of carnality and loquacity, see Newman 1995 (22–25) and Camille (70) who alert us to the powers of the mouth as a dangerous liminal zone.

[41] Beyond the appointed time, she would slump down, lean against the wall, and her face and hands would turn livid (28).

[42] Margaret of Ypres (Thomas de Cantimpré 1996, 40–41).

[43] Yvette of Huy (Hugh of Floreffe, 60).

[44] Christina the Astonishing (Thomas de Cantimpré 1999b, 20, 37, 40, 44). She lived for nine years as a recluse with Yvette of Huy.

liminality can also be observed with the Belgian beguines who enter-
tained active contacts with their lay and clerical spiritual interlocu-
tors. Even a recluse like Yvette of Huy could lead a kind of social life
with her advisors and the increasing number of persons who settled
their own cells close to hers.[45] Their physical location at the
periphery between two worlds corresponds to the beguines' social
status, to their position as non-cloistered and semi-secular religious
women. It also corresponds to the extramural position of hospitals
and hospices usually situated at the edges of the town and marking
their boundaries.[46]

Paradox is the key word which seems to define the attitude of
these women toward asceticism and suffering. Mortification was not
sought for itself but as a route to a higher good, to the perfect joy
which is the constant desire of the mystics, unity with the divine
Beloved (9:39; 9:44; 9:47).[47] This is why the sicknesses that often
struck them were received with fortitude and even with gratitude, as
gifts. These afflictions were signs that their desire to share Christ's
martyrdom had been fulfilled[48] and they validated their roles as inter-
cessors for the redemption of souls.[49] The mystic's spirit of sacrifice
found its reward in the consoling interventions of Christ or the
Virgin. A recurring detail, often associated with the descriptions of
the mystics' demonstrations of asceticism, confirms that their main
intention was not the exaltation of suffering and the debasing of the
body. In many cases, whatever the severity of the fasting or the
tortures inflicted, the body was said to be unharmed. Christina the
Astonishing's extraordinary adventures did not leave traces of
wounds.[50] Marie d'Oignies' ascetic performances were constantly
comforted by grace: she did not feel the pain of a self-inflicted
wound,[51] felt stronger when she fasted,[52] spent nights in vigils

---

[45] Yvette of Huy (Hugh of Floreffe, 82–83). We agree with Bynum (1991, 68–74) on
the division between innerwordly-active asceticism of southern pious women and
world-fleeing contemplative northern mystics.
[46] Gilchrist, 46–49.
[47] Expressions of that joy in Lutgard of Aywières (Thomas de Cantimpré 1991, 36,
49, 61); Yvette of Huy (Hugh of Floreffe, 108); Margaret of Ypres (Jacques de
Vitry, 36, 45); Christina the Astonishing (Thomas de Cantimpré 1999b, 47, 63).
[48] This is a central theme in Margaret Ebner's experience as well as in late medieval
English mystics (Ross).
[49] Newman 1995, 119–22.
[50] Christina the Astonishing (Thomas de Cantimpré 1999b, 21, 22, 23).
[51] Marie d'Oignies (Jacques de Vitry, 63).
[52] *Ibid.*, 65.

without any harm to her body[53] and was invigorated by her abundant tears.[54] Douceline's vita is similar in this respect, her "normal" physical suffering being mentioned almost in passing (10:7) and the tortures she endured while in ecstasy were unfelt until she returned to herself.

This series of paradoxes reveals the underlying motivation of mortification as an efficient way, through practices of control over the body, of accessing a form of power which itself manifests the type of reversal that is proper to mystic experience. On the one hand this power comes from being able to conquer the basic needs of one's body, to reach that state of virginal purity which in itself possesses a quasi-magical property as Douceline's Life mentions explicitly, stating that, having served God with purity, "she rightly deserved the visits and consolations of the angels" (10:5).[55] On the other hand, it comes from being able to abandon oneself to God's will, to totally lose any form of control and become the object of the ecstatic trance.[56] The supernatural powers manifested by the mystic's body legitimized her sacrifice and proved it successful. These powers applied to herself through her ravishments and ecstasies, and to others through the miracles she performed. Both forms of spiritual achievement are Douceline's hallmark. The details of her asceticism do not diverge notably from the common pattern. Her mystic career flowered and gained recognition through the intensity and frequency of her raptures and levitations, and her miracles. Here again, there is nothing markedly different from other lives that describe the same signs of the powers acquired by the mystic. Along with ecstatic ravishments and miracles, the usual manifestations are the visions and revelations she receives or performs, and the ability to prophesy, all elements which are meant to confirm her spiritual stature and legitimize her role as guide and advisor. In other words, they allow

---

53 *Ibid.*, 75.
54 *Ibid.*, 46. Lutgard of Aywières also felt stronger when she fasted (Thomas de Cantimpré 1991, 46).
55 Newman 1995, 23, 30–31.
56 Without excluding the sense of control experienced over themselves and their entourage as a parallel with contemporary anorexia would suggest, we are here speaking of a form of spiritual power that manifests itself through the body and the cult of relics (Vauchez 1981, 499; Bynum 1987, 255; Finke 1993, 38–42). About the power given to the mystic according to merits, see Heffernan (156), legitimizing their quest for purity (McNamara 1993 in Wiethaus 1993, 15–17).

her to perform the role of preacher, a role normally inaccessible to a lay person, let alone a woman.

Douceline's visions and manifestations of miraculous powers

The apparitions Douceline received at the beginning of her religious life played a determining role in shaping her Franciscan orientation. It was the encounter with two women and a little girl at Hyères which made her determined to establish her own institution and to wear the same type of clothing, reminiscent of the mantle the Virgin wore after her son's death (2:4; 2:9). Even earlier, two parallel visions had confirmed her Franciscan vocation – and the mission of her community – of service to the poor and sick. Both were visits of Christ in the guise of a sick beggar, and occurred when she was still living with her father, devoting herself to charity work. During the first, the divine beggar asked her to put her hand on his side, a request premonitory of what would be the constant painful contradiction of her life, being compelled to overcome her obsessive modesty (1:6) and to exhibit her ravished body. The second occurred in a dream she had while sleeping, overcome with the exhaustion of caring for a sick man: she saw him "enjoying himself in a wonderful meadow". Discovering him dead when she awoke, she understood that her choice of life of serving the poor and sick had been validated (1:7). Most of her visions were of the Virgin and Christ (10:8).[57] They were related to the Nativity, with images of the crib or of a ray of sunlight shining out of the Virgin's womb (10:10) or the Crucifixion, with the representation of the wounded Christ associated with its incarnation in the Eucharist (10:15), with graphic evocations of his Passion, of his bruises and wounds, "bleeding from all parts of his body" (10:13–15). The Joachimite influence on Douceline's Franciscanism appears in two visions she had of the Virgin and relate to the Holy Spirit and the symbol of lilies (10:11–12).[58] Unlike those of other mystics, the apparitions granted to Douceline were of images to be interpreted, without any explicit dialogue, either with the divinity or with dead friends or relatives asking for redeeming prayers and advising her on her afterlife.[59]

[57] She is also frequently supported by apparitions of angels. We find in other mystics's lives visions of the Virgin and Christ, apparitions of saints and angels, as well as friends or relatives asking for prayers.
[58] See discussion below, 152–53.
[59] Dauphine of Puimichel had a vision of her husband and of her aunt who explained to her how the Elect were chosen (Cambell, 175). The most interesting example of

As with many other mystics, Douceline's appearances after her
death served to confirm her status of godly woman and enabled her
to continue the work begun on earth. The stability and legitimization
of the community she founded were her main preoccupations in life;
they would also be recurrent themes of her afterlife appearances. On
several occasions her visions had contained the guarantee that her
institution would be under the protection of the Holy Trinity
(10:20–25). After her death, she first manifested herself on several
occasions to confirm her saintly status in order to validate the biography to be written about her and to support her "Order" (14:6–23),
and she also appeared to the sisters at Hyères as they commemorated
the anniversary of her death (14:24–27). Obviously we do not find
such preoccupations in the lives of other lay women who were not
invested with that kind of responsibility. Their apparitions were
usually meant to give advice, bring consolation, announce an imminent death, or convey information, as Douceline also does, about
their afterlife in heaven.[60]

The blissful experience of ecstatic ravishment which is the
common reward of spiritual devotion and ascetic dedication, was a
particularly intense phenomenon in Douceline's mysticism.[61] Its
evolution transcended her own state of union with the Divine, to be
used as a means of conveying messages to her community and
beyond. The more she progressed in her spirituality, the more
frequent and extended were her raptures (13:3), provoked by the
names of Christ, the Virgin, St. Francis or other saints (9:5), the
hearing of mass or a sermon (9:34; 9:37), receiving the Eucharist
(9:22; 9:27; 9:46),[62] or – in a true Francis-like fashion – the sight of a
flower or the song of a bird (9:19; 13:4). They could last for hours,
usually from the morning communion to evening around compline

---

a dialogue between the mystic and her vision is Constance of Rabastens whose 63
visions are a constant exchange between her and her Voice, comforting and
instructing her (see Hiver-Bérenguier). Compare also the dialogues of Elisabeth of
Schönau, Julian of Norwich and Margery Kempe.

60 Advice: Yvette of Huy (Hugh of Floreffe, 125–26), Marie d'Oignies (Jacques de
Vitry, 153 and suppl. Thomas de Cantimpré 1999a, 248–49); consolation: Marie
d'Oignies (suppl. 245–46); imminent death: Lutgard of Aywières (Thomas de
Cantimpré 1991, 112); information about afterlife: Margaret of Ypres (Thomas de
Cantimpré 1996, 63–64).

61 On the importance given to ecstasy in Franciscan devotion: Burr 1983, 31–38;
1985, 278; Lerner 1992; Ziegler in Wiethaus 1993, 112.

62 Eating is an occasion for Douceline to be reminded of Christ's spiritual meal
(9:52–54).

(9:12; 9:22) or even several days, for example at Christmas, Good Friday or the feast of the Assumption of the Virgin, in mid-August (9:46; 9:48; 13:12). Her ecstasies operated as an instrument for communicating her will to her sisters, and even for lecturing them. In one of her most dramatic sessions of ecstatic rapture, she walked, singing, into the dormitory, followed by the sisters, with their candles burning, as if they were in a procession (9:60–64). The waving of her hands around her head when she stopped was interpreted as a sign of God's benediction on their new house that was being established in Marseilles. The threats to her community, because of pressures to have her group join an established order, and because of the uncertainty of its future after her death, found convenient defences in her ecstatic visions.[63] Once, for example, she saw a golden ladder[64] coming down from the sky to the earth, with angels kneeling in front of God and the Holy Trinity, as a confirmation of heavenly support (10:21). Douceline used her ecstasies to inculcate in the sisters the importance of the preservation of their order and the necessity of keeping its unity. A vision involving the Holy Trinity led to special devotion, with prayers to the Trinity said after matins and compline (10:24). After another ecstasy, she convoked the chapter in order to advise the sisters that she had received the instruction from God that only one prioress should lead both houses, and to ask them to make a solemn promise to respect that decision (10:32).

But what marked Douceline out, secured her reputation, and attracted crowds of devotees and worshippers were her levitations. Made public by their spectacular and almost theatrical aspect, with their authenticity being carefully tested (9:16), they were directed towards communal and even political purposes. Both purposes could be intermingled, as when the Count of Artois and several clerics witnessed how, while levitating, she received the comforting reassurance, on behalf of herself and her sisters, that they would be saved (9:36–40), a confirmation reiterated during another trance on Good Friday (9:57). On the one hand, the presence of these distinguished persons gave weight to the message, on the other hand, as witnesses of God's word, they became committed to support the community.

---

63 Hugh's death must have left the community without spiritual guidance in the eyes of the authorities. The traditionally accepted date of 1285 for Hugh's death was first questioned by Albanés, who suggests 1255–56 as being more likely (l–lii). Reeves (1969, 185) supports his argument for the earlier date.
64 The biblical image of Jacob's ladder (Genesis 28:12) occurs frequently in accounts of mystic visions; see, for example, Elisabeth of Schönau (Clark, 54).

The best demonstration, however, of the convergence, through Douceline's mystical experiences, of her own preoccupations and external political issues, is the nature of her relationship with Charles of Anjou, count of Provence and king of Sicily. It was during a conflict between Charles and the Franciscans, that the countess, suffering a difficult pregnancy, saw Douceline in a dream which she had three times, was helped by her prayers and safely delivered a daughter (4:10–13).[65] Not only were the Franciscans restored to the count's good graces, but he generously provided donations to Douceline's houses (5:8). This was the beginning of an exchange where she exercised the gift of prophecy that had been granted to her in order to counsel him. When he asked her advice before accepting the kingdom of Sicily, she encouraged him to proceed but warned him against being carried away by pride (11:5), and subsequently castigated him in her letters, prophesying a reversal of fortune if he did not follow her directives (11:7–8).[66] Although she did not live to see its outcome, Douceline's prediction for Charles was to prove all too accurate (11:9).

Among the many powers acquired by – or divinely conferred on – the mystic, the ability to prophesy was closely related to her role as spiritual advisor. She not only announced events to come such as deaths, famines, slaughters or battles;[67] a recurrent motif in the Lives mentions that she is able to read thoughts and see into hearts. Since she could foresee temptations and was able to know that sins had been committed, she was in a good position to provide counselling. Evident in Douceline's Life (11:10–13), the theme is particularly significant in the Lives of the Belgian beguines because of the importance given to their pastoral role.[68] We see them bringing

---

65   There are several occurrences of the number three. See, for example, in 8:7.
66   The French were massacred in Palermo in January 1282; Sicily was eventually won by Peter of Aragon.
67   Deaths: Christina the Astonishing (Thomas de Cantimpré 1999b, 33), Lutgard of Aywières (Thomas de Cantimpré 1991, 77), Marie d'Oignies (Jacques de Vitry, 127), Dauphine of Puimichel (Cambell, 179); famines, etc: Christina the Astonishing (32–35), Lutgard of Aywières (9), Marie d'Oignies (Jacques de Vitry, 100, 125). On the definition of prophecy including "past, present and future tenses" and being "rightly so called not because it predicts the future, but rather because it reveals the hidden . . . and it deals with the present when the secrets of the heart are disclosed", based on St. Gregory's exposition of Ezekiel, see Juliana of Mont-Cornillon (Newman 1991, 54).
68   This role is particularly stressed in Yvette of Huy's Life. See Finke (in Wiethaus 1993, 31–35). We would agree with Lauwers (85–103) that the pastoral role of the

comfort to troubled souls, inciting remorse or conversion, and consoling the dying.[69] To this variety of clerical tasks, we must add their activity of counselling clerics and important people, and even providing theological advice.[70] The ability to undertake responsibilities normally prohibited to lay people, let alone women, is related to the precept that the humbled shall be exalted. Here again, our women's authority rests on supernatural gifts. Christina the Astonishing understood Latin and knew the meaning of Holy Scripture, even though she had been illiterate from birth;[71] Lutgard received the revelation of the meaning of the Psalter from the Holy Spirit so that Thomas de Cantimpré, in contrast, felt uncultivated and dull;[72] Marie d'Oignies was able to instruct Jacques de Vitry on the art of delivering a sermon.[73]

All of this applies to Douceline whose ability to instruct clerics, including a Franciscan theologian (9:29–32; 11:2), was also due to her divinely inspired knowledge of the Scripture, legitimized by Hugh himself who attested to the high quality of her mind, even if – according to the usual topos – she was "a simple, uneducated woman" (9:3). We see her described by her biographer in the performance of preaching at Easter, on Holy Thursday. She delivers a model sermon, developing a lengthy exemplum to explain the mystery of resurrection (10:27–29). She shows how a dove came to a good man who wondered how to conduct himself properly on Good Friday, collapsed nearly dead until Holy Saturday when the bird revived and flew into the air. The anecdote demonstrates how the women's exposure to preaching – and high quality preaching in the

women mystics is complementary to the priest's, but we would qualify their submission to the confessor's control. Bériou (1998) argues that the right for women to preach beyond the family circle of their children can be seen in a more prominent way by the end of the twelfth century.

[69] Comfort to troubled souls: Lutgard of Awières (Thomas de Cantimpré 1991, 81), Yvette of Huy (107); persuasion to remorse: Margaret of Ypres (Thomas de Cantimpré 1996, 27, 45), Yvette of Huy (Hugh of Floreffe, 77, 96, 98, 104, 1090–111); to conversion: Marie d'Oignies (Jacques de Vitry, 108 and suppl., Thomas de Cantimpré 1999a, 221), Dauphine of Puimichel (Cambell, 207–209); consolation to the dying: Christina the Astonishing (Thomas de Cantimpré 1999b, 40), Dauphine of Puimichel (Cambell, 179).

[70] Counseling: Dauphine of Puimichel (Cambell, 177); theological advice: Margaret of Ypres (Thomas de Cantimpré 1996, 47), Marie d'Oignies (Jacques de Vitry, 119–20), Dauphine of Puimichel (Cambell, 205–207).

[71] Christina the Astonishing (Thomas de Cantimpré 1999b, 38).

[72] Lutgard (Thomas de Cantimpré 1991, 35, 52–59, 73).

[73] Marie d'Oignies (Jacques de Vitry, 121–122).

case of Douceline's brother – could provide them with adequate training in the art of sermon.[74] Where Douceline departs from other beguines, is once again in her supervisory functions over the community; her position gave her not only the power to instruct and admonish, but also the authority to punish.[75] She is presented as a mix of harshness and gentleness (6:6–11). The examples of her severity are not without violence, as when she beat the little seven-year-old girl who had looked at men working (6:5), but the violence is tempered by mentions of her sweetness when the sinner showed repentance (6:11).

Like the physical punishments she personally administered, most of Douceline's miraculous cures entailed close physical contact.[76] The few examples which do not imply physical contact address what we might now label as psychological interventions: bringing a malicious woman to repentance (9:11), stopping a quarrel in invoking the Virgin (12:9), curing a fit of madness when she was invoked by its victim after her death (15:33–34), or inflicting pain on a man who was about to betray a vow, healing him when he changed his mind (15:36–39). Even in this case, however, her action might require direct contact, for example when a man who was thought to be out of his mind because of his evil deeds, returned to God as soon as his parents placed a relic of the saint in his clothing (15:30–31). In the more usual cases of physical illnesses, either the sick person touched Douceline, kissing the soles of her feet while she levitated, or holding her hands (9:9; 12:5), or more often, she touched the part of the body to be cured (12:2; 12:6; 12:13; 12:24; 12:25).[77] A miracle involving touching took place during the ritual washing of feet on Holy Thursday when Douceline, humbly joining her sisters in washing and kissing the feet of the others, cured a mortal affliction (12:8). A variant occurred when the sick person came into contact with something she had herself touched, for example when Rixende

---

74 McDonnell (343, 400): about preaching as a teaching tool for women, and on popular religious literature accessible to women. The image of the resurgent dove in Douceline's sermon is echoed in the frequent references to "the wings of St. Francis" throughout the text (9:39; 9:57; 10:35 ff).

75 Christina the Astonishing, for example, admonishes priests in secret (Thomas de Cantimpré 1999b, 38), and reprimands the Count of Looz when he does something unjust (39).

76 Carozzi 1976, 265. We understand that she began performing miracles early in her life, even before the move to Marseilles (12:6).

77 The beneficiary could be an animal, like the dying horse brought back to health when she touched it (12:3).

du Puget washed her ailing eyes with wine from her cup: "wine that the Saint's lips had touched" (12:6). Many of her posthumous miracles were ways of having her touch the sufferer, either with her finger kept as a relic in a silver reliquary (15:15; 15:19), or with water in which her finger had soaked (15:21; 15:29). Nor did death prevent Douceline from performing her usual touching of the sick body-part. After having invoked her, a blind woman felt a hand on her eyes and was able to see again and, as we have seen, a young sister, sick in bed, was cured when Douceline appeared to her and gently rubbed her feet (15:12; 14:10).

Some cases demonstrate the sacrificial aspect of a miraculous cure, when something is asked in exchange, such as a child's weight in wax, wax in the shape of eyes, candles, or the promise to enter the Franciscan Order or the Roubaud community (15:2; 15:10; 15:35–39; 15:9; 15:17).[78] Once again, the community's survival and development are central concerns, as three of Douceline's posthumous interventions show; each incident has crucial consequences for her status as a saint and, consequently, for the legitimacy of her foundations. The first one takes place when the carefully staged apparition of Douceline puts an end to a dispute about her sainthood which was dangerously dividing the sisters (14:6–23). The circumstances of the event are in themselves telling, since it occurs precisely when Philippine was writing her Life, and when one of the sisters had raised doubts about the sainthood of their founder. It is in that context that the sister mentioned above was cured of her sickness. The second one concerns Maragde Porcellet, Philippine's niece, an aspect which deserves consideration, as does the kind of ailment affecting her. She was the object of two interventions for problems with her voice, impairing her speech or preventing her from speaking (15:22–28). If the first cure is a classic case of healing severe hiccups by drinking water, in this case water in which the finger of the saint had been bathed, the second parallels the story of the dispute among the sisters. It occurred the very day when the Life of the saint was to be read aloud for the first time at the annual celebration in her honour. Maragde was able to recover her voice for that occasion but she lost it once again after that for a while, a fact that underlines the relationship between the problems affecting the speech of the sister closest to Philippine and the validation of the task undertaken by Philippine the biographer.

---

[78] Vauchez 1981, 530–36.

One of the more historically interesting miracles performed by Douceline is her cure of a child's scrofula (12:24). The power of healing this inflammation of the neck glands accompanied by painful abscesses, by touching the sick part of the body, was traditionally the exclusive prerogative of the king of France, bestowed upon him during the anointment with sacred oil at his coronation. Geneviève Brunel-Lobrichon stresses that this is a unique case of a woman – a lay woman – touching and healing the scrofula.[79] One cannot help but relate this miracle to others involving pregnant women and newborn babies. We know the beneficial consequences of Douceline's intervention with the countess of Provence. Three other miracles, performed after her death, are an indication of Douceline's power to play with life and death, at least as Philippine presents them: she provides a son to a baron of Provence and his wife, a child so intelligent that "he appeared to be a special gift from God"; she then, apparently, brings his brother back from the dead (15:2–3).[80] The third example, of another successful pregnancy, is told with details suggesting the same kind of godlike powers. Douceline appears to the mother, accompanied by twelve sisters of Roubaud – the number of Christ's apostles – and speaks to her with words evoking the Annunciation: "I have come to tell you that you are carrying a son who will bring you joy" (15:5–7).

The physicality of Douceline's interventions, even after her death, shows the significance given to the body in her spiritual journey. In a more consistent way than in other mystic Lives, Douceline's body subsumes all the paradoxes and opposing values inherent in her mysticism. The constraints she imposed on her body by the obliteration of its needs contrast with its increasing sensibility. Her ever more frequent and longer raptures were often initiated by physical, acoustic or optical sensations like listening to discourses about God, hearing liturgical chant or birds singing (9:18–19). At the end of her life, the sight of a flower, a fruit, or a bird was enough to provoke a rapture (13:4) as if her extreme sensitivity to the created world connected her to the supernatural.[81] In a clear manifestation of the

---

[79] Brunel-Lobrichon 1988a, 51.

[80] Miracles involving pregnant mothers in Vauchez 1981, 550. There is an echo here of "the Marseilles miracle" attributed, in *The Golden Legend*, to Mary Magdalene; a pagan ruler's wife conceives a son. The same account also describes the Magdalene's levitation while engaged in mystical contemplation (Ludwig Jansen 2000, 191). Another kind of miracle Douceline performed also deals with the notion of fecundity, when she filled up the barrel of flour which was empty (12:26).

[81] Carozzi 1975, 188.

spiritual powers conferred by the conquest of her physical needs, her body becomes the elected channel of her communication with God. Time and time again, the outward signs of this election are described with the same terms: while her body suddenly rises up, she becomes "bright red and was all afire" (9:32; 9:47).[82] Her state of pure spirituality, the outcome of her complete abandonment of physicality, is made manifest in a concretely physical way, an embodiment of the naturalistic theology most explicitly formulated by St. Francis: the "whole world was like a representation of God; everything she saw represented her Lord to her, and by her love, she found God in all things" (8:2).

As we have seen, eating and drinking could be sources of spiritual meditation and ecstasy, a form of prayer, for Douceline. This Franciscan attention to the body and to the materiality of the Creation finds a striking expression in a dream a pious countess had of Douceline (10:9). The saint appeared to her and she saw oil "like gold, flowing from the holy mother's breast", a vision identifying Douceline with "Jesus as Mother", this deity whose flesh was food.[83] The fact that this oil was burned in a lamp on the altar of the Virgin extends the identification to the Holy Mother. This fusion translates itself for her into physical manifestations of pain, feeling for example "as if all the bones in her body had been pierced" (9:28), with the multiplication of the signs of her exhaustion as a consequence: she almost collapses (9:21), seems to expire (9:48), appears dead (9:50) or utters cries of sorrow (9:49). But pain transforms itself into the spiritual joy which gives brilliance to her face, her pale cheeks burning. The metaphor of drunkenness and "spiritual intoxication" conveys the sense of the aesthete's loss of control of over her body (9:65) which manifests itself also in her insensibility during her ecstasies. There is a sort of sadistic overindulgence in the realistic descriptions of tortures inflicted upon her by sceptical witnesses who wanted to test the authenticity of her ravishment, like pricking her with iron spikes, poking needles under her fingernails, or pouring melted lead on her feet (9:16). She suffered no pain from any of these assaults, feeling her injuries only when she returned to normality. The tortures were justified by the need to authenticate Douceline's raptures and levitations as true and genuine expressions of her divine election, along with other ways of proving them, such as mentioning

---

82 Vauchez 1981, 499–500 and 509–10: sainthood is an energy which manifests itself on the body of the saint and particularly on the face.

83 Bynum 1982 and 1987, 272–75.

the names of the witnesses and measuring the distance between the ground and her feet. Philippine, although she clearly supports the need for evidence, seems to distance herself from the voyeuristic abuse performed by well-intentioned worshippers who "tested her unscrupulously in painful ways" (9:35).

It was also with self-inflicted physical pain that Douceline tried, unsuccessfully, to overcome these intermittent losses of control of her body during her raptures. She resented being exposed to the public eye in such a condition, and secretly wounded herself, piercing her hands with needles during masses or sermons – a sort of self-inflicted stigmata – hoping that suffering would prevent her from being ravished (9:31; 34; 37).[84] She was, moreover, the object of violence and aggression from adoring crowds, endangering her by wanting to touch her (9:24). This public exposure confronted her with what seems to be the most painful contradiction of her vocation. Her dedication to humility conflicted with the veneration she received from prelates and other important people. It compelled her to despise honours and praise (4:3), to become disturbed if people knelt before her (4:4–6) and, consequently, forced her to try to avoid what she was yearning for, her complete spiritual rapture. (9:26–28).[85] This tension between self-effacing humility and the manifestation of divine grace is inherent in the vocation of the mystic. Also common is the spectacular display of these manifestations, their "theatricalization". Her vita chronicles an increasing dramatization of Douceline's carefully crafted performances, rendered with a luxury of details by Philippine when they were related to important issues such as the destiny of the community. A common motif of pious women's vitae is loud weeping and cries "for the sorrow of the Virgin and her son", that can be heard from far (9:49).[86]

One of these "staged" performances deserves to be recounted in detail because it occurred at the time of the foundation of the house in Marseilles, and involved the whole community (9:59–64). After a day spent in ecstasy on the eve of the Ascension of Jesus Christ, she began walking, followed by the sisters like in a procession, singing an

84 These self-inflicted wounds can be related to the effect on Douceline of Francis' stigmata (9:42, 43, 44) and to her visions of a bleeding Christ "covered with bruises" with wounds in his hands and side (10:14, 15).

85 Carozzi 1975, 175–77.

86 For other examples in Belgian beguines, see Marie d'Oignies (Jacques de Vitry, 45–46; 58) and Lutgard (Thomas de Cantimpré 1991, 49). Lutgard also levitated "two cubits from the earth" (29).

other-worldly song and uttering words they could not understand. After a while she stopped, raised her arm circling around her head "to indicate the diadem of God's great magnificence", a gesture that the sisters all understood as a sign that their house was blessed.[87] As we see, this quasi-liturgical dramatization of reassurances about the future of the Roubaud community, in this world and the other, was accompanied by other ritualizations such as the vow Douceline required from the sisters to maintain the integrity and the unity of the Order (10:32). In the manner of a feudal overlord Douceline asked them to swear an oath, "one after the other . . . with their hands between hers".

Already manifest during her life, the tension between the private saintly woman and the sacred icon into which she had been transformed, was to become particularly acute at the time of her death and during her funerals. The tumult of the crowd wanting to touch her, to grab something of her as a relic, was such that three tunics covering her corpse were successively torn to pieces and she was almost dismembered in spite of the civic force called to control the crowds (13:16–21). There is nothing exceptional in the coveting of relics.[88] The Lives of Lutgard of Aywières and Marie d'Oignies give striking examples of the practice of dismembering a saintly body as a sign of veneration.[89] Once again, what happened in Douceline's case is consistent with the other manifestations of her sainthood and with her status in the community. She was not the object of controlled veneration within the institution, but became the prey of an almost uncontrollable mob. Douceline's funerals, the first following her death and the two subsequent translations of her body, echo scenes in

---

[87] See also 9:39 and 9:55 where Douceline, levitating with her arms stretched out in a cross, crying and weeping, seems to re-enact Christ's Passion. These dramatizations can be related to Elizabeth of Spalbeeck's performances of the Passion analysed in Simons and Ziegler.

[88] Vauchez 1981, 272–80 and 501–507. About the trade and "commodification" of relics, see Geary 1978 and 1986.

[89] Even before Lutgard died, Thomas de Cantimpré pleaded with the sisters that if he were not present at her death, they would amputate her hand and keep it as a sacred memorial of her. In fact, when she died, some lay brothers cut off a finger of her right hand and extracted sixteen teeth. Thomas subsequently negotiated with the abbess for possession of the finger in exchange for the promise that he would write her Life (Thomas de Cantimpré 1991, 108–109). In Marie's case, the negotiation took place with her dead body itself when the Prior stole the corpse with some thieves, and tried unsuccessfully to remove her clenched teeth. When he prayed to her to give him some of her teeth as solace for his sorrows, the lifeless corpse "opened its mouth and, on its own accord, shook out seven teeth into the hand of the prior" (Thomas de Cantimpré 1991, 237–38).

her life, when the populace massed around her during her ecstasies and levitations, hoping to touch her (9:24). She was the passive object of the people's gaze and assault, subject to the ambivalent curiosity and possessive love of the town.

Like her contacts with the wider community, the expression of Douceline's spiritual powers in her relationships with the ladies of Roubaud were also marked by paradox. Humility is the key word for her own behaviour as well as for the conduct she wanted to impose on them (4:4–6); the very foundation of her institution was meant to provoke scorn and disdain (4:1–2). This is why she chose the name of beguine and refused to allow her ladies to have a church built, or "to acquire skill in letters or to sing the office, or to have anything that would raise them too high" (4:4). As a demonstration of her own humility she selected one of them, Philippine Porcellet, as her personal "prioress" to whom she would submit and whom she would obey (4:9). However, obedience was also expected from Douceline's ladies; any new recruit made a vow to obey her (6:1) and Philippine records that she was "fearsome in her reprimands and punishments" (6:11). Their rapport was indeed more hierarchical than congenial: "these good women learned the holy lessons she taught them willingly. . . . They lived in great fear of Our Lord, and in obedience to the holy mother" (3:9). As we have seen, in her determination to instruct her ladies, the sweetness of positive reinforcement barely masks the severity of her chastisement. She reproduced with them the combination of love and violence she experienced from her devotees. Even in her most humbly communal interactions with her ladies, such as the two occasions where she is shown joining in washing the feet of the community on Holy Thursday, Douceline's difference is underlined: she uses the first occasion to deliver a masterful sermon (10:26–29) and the second to perform a miracle (12:8). Even those sisters who were closest to her, like those outside the fence of lilies in her vision, were excluded from the innermost circle (10:12). Constantly aware of her responsibility and obligations as the founder of the institution, and possessed of spectacular powers which marked her as God's chosen one, she remained isolated by a spiritual grace that could not be shared with them, but only admired with wonder.

Yet the development of her own mystical link with the divine was not the ultimate object of her ecstatic episodes. In her raptures and levitations, or in her miraculous interventions, the interests of her community were at the forefront. Nor can identification between her personal evolution and the strength of the Roubaud order be dissociated from the larger religious and political context that guaranteed its survival. More precisely, the existence and permanence of the beguines was closely linked to the fluctuating fortunes of the Franciscan order.

The Beguines of Roubaud and Douceline's Theology

Douceline's central concern for confirming the legitimacy of the institution and guaranteeing its future was certainly shared by Philippine of Porcellet, as prioress of the houses after her, and provided one of the motivations for the writing of the saint's biography. We have seen that many ecstatic episodes were related to this issue as well as some posthumous interventions of Douceline. Her apparitions to the sisters are explicit in this respect. They took place at key moments: when doubts were raised about Douceline's sainthood, doubts which affected the Life itself, which was in the process of being composed, when the Life was to be read for the first time (15:24), or when a celebration was taking place honouring her memory (14:24–26). In a vision, one of the beguines sees one of her sisters who had just died, arriving in Paradise where her community and her habit are questioned by a gathering of saints. The order is justified and supported by Jesus Christ himself who, echoing the words of the mysterious ladies on the road near Hyères (2:4), confirms that she belongs to an order he loves (14:28–31). Having reported this scene, Philippine cannot help involving herself and the whole group, using the first-person plural. In one of her few interventions, the biographer insists that their founder's promise that the community cannot disappear will be fulfilled, thanks to God's help (14:32–33).

The questions asked by the saints raise the very issue that confronted Douceline and the ladies of Roubaud: as followers of St. Francis, why did they not simply join the Franciscan order of the Poor Clares?[90] As we have seen, the larger issue at stake was the status of the beguines, especially in southern France where the control of the orthodoxy of lay people was a great concern for the Church. Douceline who, according to Philippine, was the first beguine and the originator of the movement in this area, was well aware of the ambivalence of the hierarchy toward them, and her choice was an informed one (2:11). Even before her conversion and decision to found a community, she had led a life of devotion, asceticism and service to the sick and poor, a natural consequence of the

---

90 They were already installed in Southern France at Hugh's death. About the date of the first sisters of St. Clare in Provence, see Brunel-Lobrichon 1988b, 261–80.

Franciscan orientation of her family. Already, she was the leader of a group of women who followed her example (2:2), attracted also, perhaps, by the power of Hugh's preaching (3:2–3).[91] The vita is unclear on the exact succession of events which led her to apply to herself and the community she wanted to organize the name of beguines. We are told about the miraculous encounter, echoing that of Francis, which determined her decision, and the fact that it took place at a time when Hugh was in Paris. There is a certain imprecision in the chronology: the encounter with the holy ladies occurred on a road near Hyères, but we know that Douceline stayed in a Minorite convent in Genoa during her brother's absence. What may be deduced, however, is that she might have heard about the northern beguines from Hugh on his return from Paris, and that their example may have inspired her and enticed her to share with him what had happened. The vita does make clear that before these two events – Hugh's journey and Douceline's encounter with the ladies – no one had heard the word beguine in Provence (2:2), and that she henceforth determined to make the name her own. She deliberately reversed a term which had some taint of contempt[92] into a name of praise: "she would say that the name of beguine pleased her greatly and that she held it in great esteem because it was humble and scorned by the world's pride" (4:2).

The ladies of Roubaud shared the two main characteristics of northern beguines: their consecration to a life of chastity and charity, and the fact that they did not follow a recognized monastic rule. The vita describes how Douceline, demonstrating the organizational skills evident in other aspects of her direction of the houses, managed social service. She "employed women who went out looking for the poor" who were housed in lodgings at this effect (8:4), and had beds available at the Roubaud houses for them (8:5). Like the northern beguines, because of their intermediary status, the ladies were not subject to close male control and they enjoyed a certain amount of self-governance, even if they were usually placed under the guidance of a clerical mentor. The Lives of Marie d'Oignies and Lutgard of Aywières show that Jacques de Vitry and Thomas de Cantimpré were more spiritual partners than figures of authority. Douceline's deal-

---

91 On the importance and influence of the preaching concerning St. Francis, and his status as second Christ, see Bériou 1990, 537–38. Preaching about poverty was also related to the strong presence of the Waldensians in southern France during the thirteenth century (Dossat).

92 See the discussion of the term in the Introduction above, 8–10.

ings with male influence were somewhat more complex; the most influential men in her life were her father and her brother, Hugh of Digne. In spite of her vow of obedience to Brother Jaucelin, provincial minister of the Friars Minor (4:9), she seemed to consider herself as his equal, having developed the same kind of spiritual friendship with this confidant of her more secret revelations (10:6) as that established between the Belgian beguines and their clerical companions (10:3). Placed in the position of an obedient daughter, sister and pious devotee by society and by her own sense of humility, Douceline emerges, nonetheless, as a strong woman who is actually in control of male power. Not only does she exert her leadership over her institutions and her authority over the sisters, but she is also in a position to influence their male relatives and admirers, often members of important aristocratic families, as in the role she played in the political decision-making of the count of Provence.

Her relationship with the male models provided by her family was more complex. Her first acquaintance with lay practices of devotion came from her parents who used to assist the poor (1:1), but since her mother died when she was still a child, the meaningful example for her was her father who introduced her to the service of the poor and the sick (1:5). The Franciscan model of devotion – Douceline's father was also a wealthy merchant – was personified by her brother, Hugh of Digne.[93] First-hand information on Hugh comes from two sources. The most detailed testimony is contained in Salimbene de Adam's chronicle, an account of the Italian Franciscan's meeting with him at Hyères in 1248. The other can be found in Joinville's biography of Saint Louis. The king had heard about Brother Hugh's reputation as a preacher and wanted to meet him during a brief visit to Hyères.[94] The friar spoke with his usual uncompromising severity, warning the king that the only means to hold his kingdom together was to maintain justice. He scolded monks who spent their time at the king's court, enjoying its luxury when they should stay in their monasteries, preoccupied only by thoughts of their salvation. Applying the lesson to himself, Hugh stayed just one day with the king, who was eager for his company during his time in Hyères. In Hugh's inflexibility we

---

[93] We know that St. Francis travelled in Provence – perhaps on his way to Compostella – between 1211 and 1214 (Durieux, 80).

[94] Joinville, *Vie de Saint Louis*, 327–29. It was the same year (1254) that Gerard of Borgo San Donnino published the *Eternal Evangel* which was declared heretical because of an interpretation of the Joachimite Third Age that contradicted the authority of the Old and New Testaments (Reeves 1969, 59–65).

recognize Douceline's own sense of strict discipline. Salimbene records Hugh's trenchant indictment of the luxury and idleness of the cardinals at the Council of Lyons and both Joinville and Salimbene report the popularity of his preaching, with descriptions of the crowds attending his sermons trembling when he spoke of the pains of hell, "his voice like a trumpet or thunder".[95] We will return later to consider his other way of spreading the doctrine, through private teaching to groups of lay people gathered in his chambers.[96] Salimbene's own perception of Hugh was not without ambivalence. He admired his scholarship and mastery of *disputatio*, but was cautious about Hugh's more pronounced Joachimite orientations.[97]

One episode of Hugh's career will help us to understand the part he must have played in the foundation and preservation of Douceline's community and the reasons for her choice. Our informant will again be Salimbene who relates how Hugh had been present at the foundation of the Order of the Sack. Its first adherents, beggars clad in multicoloured robes "like those worn in the old days by the servants of the Order of St. Clare", were jokingly called by the Friars Minor of Provence "wild men of the woods" because they had been inspired by the text of Hugh's sermon: "Go to the woods and learn to eat roots, for tribulations are at hand."[98] The Brethren of the Sack represented a return to a literalist early Franciscan behaviour that provoked the antagonism of many in the order itself, and led to their persecution and prohibition by Pope Honorius IV in 1286.[99] They also justified their form of religious life as an answer to the Joachimite call for renewal in the expectation of the millennium, the time of "tribulations" referred to in Hugh's precept.

What emerges from the anecdote is how Hugh's Joachimite ideology, scholarship and charisma as a preacher, conferred on him a special place in the Franciscan order, and identified him with its Spiritual fringe. While remaining a Friar himself – with privileged status, for example, the ability to receive new Brothers – he certainly favoured religious communities which responded to his views and upon which he could have an impact.[100] However, his interaction with Douceline seems to have developed over time from his total care of

95   Salimbene 217, 226.
96   Salimbene, 228.
97   Salimbene, 222, 228–47.
98   Salimbene, 248.
99   Salimbene, 249, 255–93; Goodich, 198–202.
100   Salimbene, 247.

her religious direction, to her partnership with him, and finally, to her complete autonomy. When he made his journey to Paris, he was the one who decided that she would stay with the Franciscan nuns in Genoa and not one of the convents in Provence which had accepted her (2:7). The incident is significant because his absence and her stay in a women's community must have taken place after the vision of the three ladies that induced Douceline to follow their example and before her decision to found her own institution (2:3–8). The vita suggests a complete harmony between the sister who had made her own decision to change her life and the brother who supported her in the choice of not entering a recognized order (2:7–8). As in the case of his sympathies for the Order of the Sack, we may imagine that Hugh was more comfortable with an organization which was directly under his influence and closer to his Joachimite ideal of monastic life as he promoted it in the Hyères sermon to St. Louis.[101]

Douceline made her plan public during another sermon her brother preached in Hyères and from this point he acted as the community's spiritual mentor. He received Douceline's vow of poverty when, emulating Francis, she "renounced all the treasures and riches of her father" (5:3) but applied the Franciscan doctrine of forbidding the sisters to beg and prompted them to practise moderation (5:10–11). He does not seem to have interfered in the direction of the houses, where Douceline appears to have enjoyed complete autonomy. However, she invoked his authority as co-founder at the end of her life, when she was preoccupied with concerns for the future unity and survival of the community (10:33–37). On her brother's death, her recourse in distress was the Virgin, her constant model and inspiration since her first decision to lead a religious life (10:16). As we shall see, her theological doctrine was less an *imitatio Christi* than an imitation of and even identification with the Virgin. Douceline asserted, when she decided to gather a group of lay women around her and to claim for them the name of "beguines", that the first beguine had been Mary (2:11).

Following a way of life modelled on the northern beguines might not have been an option for her if she wanted to locate her community close to her brother, in a period when new orders were not

---

101 Carozzi (1973, 275) reminds us that Hugh did not want the Brothers of the Sack to adopt a rule. See Burr (1983, 30–38) about the Joachimite "seraphic order" characterized not by an institution but a mode of activity modelled on the "seraphim", St. Francis.

allowed and the Poor Clares were not yet installed in southern France. The other reasons Douceline gave for choosing that direction imply an unambiguous criticism of traditional monastic life. She expressed her reservations under the guise of humility: being a beguine was the best way to humble oneself by avoiding praises and honours. Her daughters would remain simple and not elevate themselves in acquiring knowledge; they would not possess their own church and not indulge in the chanting of offices (4:4). Yet the ladies of Roubaud differed in many ways from the Belgian beguines. The most significant contrast is in the quasi-monastic organization of Douceline's community. Marie d'Oignies, Lutgard of Aywières and others truly lived among the world. Christina of Saint-Trond stayed with her sisters, Margaret of Ypres shared a family life that was a source of tensions particularly with her mother because of the excessive time she spent in prayers at the expense of domestic tasks.[102] Even Yvette of Huy, whose fame attracted many recluses around her own cell, and who exercised a spiritual leadership over them, did not play the role of head of an institution which Douceline performed.

Her sense of responsibility must have been fostered by the number of women who immediately followed her public decision to devote her life to Christ and his mother: as we have seen 131 disciples made a vow of virginity and 81 others committed themselves to chastity, among them her two nieces (3:1). At first, many were attracted to a religious life by Hugh's preaching, and then by Douceline's reputation for sainthood (3:1–3). With her brother's advice, she devised an organizational rule for both houses and even for the beguines who lived by themselves in surrounding streets in Hyères and Marseilles (3:5; 6:1).[103] There were clearly at least two categories of beguines: those who were not enclosed in the premises of the community and those who lived within the houses, among whom some – the most perfect – belonged to the inner circle. To all of them, Douceline was "guide and mistress", the text tells us twice (4:1; 6:1) and Philippine regularly applies the term "convent" to the community and "prioress" to their leader. As was the case with other groups of beguines, vows were not necessarily made for life and the community attracted married women as well as virgins and widows, the main difference with northern beguines being the social background

---

102 Margaret of Ypres (Thomas de Cantimpré 1996, 30).
103 The first document mentioning a Franciscan establishment in Marseilles is dated as early as 18 May 1243 (see Baratier 1973b, 181 and 190–91, for the exact location of Douceline's houses).

of the recruits (3:5). While the Flemish women usually belonged to the urban middle class, many of the ladies of Roubaud – among them Philippine Porcellet – were from the most important aristocratic families in Provence.

Indeed, having the right connections played a crucial role in the community's survival, combined with Douceline's own stature. After Hugh's death ca. 1255–56, she had to face threats against her institution and pressures to join an official order, but she managed to obtain the support of John of Parma, General Minister of the Franciscan Order and close friend of her brother.[104] His backing gave her the fortitude she needed in overcoming the difficulties of establishing a house in Marseilles (10:17–19). When Philippine became prioress, her wealth allowed her to purchase land in order to secure the establishment.[105] Conscious that the uncertainty of its status was dangerous in the long term, Douceline was particularly worried by what would happen after her death. She was well aware that the so-called rule she had devised had no binding power and therefore she admonished her daughters to consolidate their union around a higher link, Christ's love (10:25; 10:30–35). She also organized, in a series of quasi-liturgical dramatized sessions of ecstatic revelations, an election protocol for the prioress in charge of both houses (10:32). In addition to the internal weakness of an institution divided into two establishments, threats came from outside, first at the end of the century around the spiritual trend and the suspicions of heterodoxy against Peter John Olivi, then with John XXII's decrees against beguines in 1311.[106] Douceline's concern was certainly justified, for, as we have seen, despite all her efforts, the house at Roubaud was closed in 1414 and all of its goods, including *le livre de leur sainte mère*, were passed to the congregation of Friars Minor in Marseilles.[107] The role that the Franciscans were to play in the future of the Roubaud community, as well as the prestige the order would receive from her status of sainthood, were foreshadowed at the time of her death and at her funerals. Present at her death and keeping watch over her all night, they directed the organization of the

---

104 On the suspicion raised by the groups of pious women who could fit neither among the laity nor the religious orders, see Lauwers, 71–78. For the pressures upon them to embrace a cloistered rule, McNamara 1991 in Blumenfeld-Kosinski and Szell, 208–12. In 1254 two Poor Clares came from Assisi in order to organize a community in Marseilles (Baratier 1973b, 187).
105 Albanés, Pièces Justificatives, 265–68.
106 See Introduction, 13.
107 Albanés, xiv; Introduction, 12.

ceremonies (13:12; 13:15). Her body was carried in their church (13:19) where they placed her with her brother, leading processions honouring her (13:22). One year later, they presided over the translation of her body in a marble tomb (14:3; 14:5), then in October 1278, her remains and Hugh's were transferred in great solemnity to the brothers' new church (14:34–36).

Along with Douceline's pseudo-monastic way of organizing religious women, there were more traditional groups of beguines – and lay religious men as well – in southern France, living in the world and attracted to the pursuit of a spiritual life. They are well documented in connection with the influence and writings of Peter-John Olivi who was active in Provence and Languedoc around 1280.[108] His commentaries on the Apocalypse, particularly the *Lectura super Apocalipsim*, won him a leading position among the Spiritual Franciscans.[109] His teaching was followed by numerous devout people, to whom he directed his vernacular works, the *Informatio Petri Johannis*, the *Remedia contre tentationes spirituales*, and the *Miles armatus*.[110] Olivi was a controversial figure, partly because of his Joachimite leanings, but mostly because of his support of extreme poverty.[111] A commission, appointed by Pope John XXII to examine his theology, issued a formal condemnation in October 1326.[112] The groups of men and women who used to meet together for reading and commenting on spiritual writings became more and more suspect because of their links with the Spiritual fringe of the Franciscans, mostly through Olivi's works.[113] At the turn of the fourteenth century, their meetings were banned and some of them were tried by the Inquisition.[114] The best documented example is the visionary Prous Boneta who had her first vision of Christ at Olivi's tomb and was imprisoned in 1328.[115] This did not mean the end of lay religiosity in southern France. The Franciscan influence remained strong

---

108 McDonnell 433; Manselli 1989, 33–35: he died and was buried in Narbonne on 14 March, 1298.
109 Burr 1985; Manselli 1989; Barone. Dauphine of Puimichel was closely linked with the Spirituals: Vauchez 1987b, 197.
110 Manselli 1976.
111 Manselli 1989, 85; Burr 1989b; Barone, 56.
112 Manselli 1989, 112.
113 Manselli 1989, 36–37, 74–76, 152–53, 214–21; Emmerson and Herzman, 83–84.
114 Manselli 1989, 37 and 141, concerning the role of Bernard Gui who attacked them in his *Practica inquisitionis*.
115 Manselli 1989, 196–202, who gives other examples.

and the Spiritual, Joachimite trend, continued to be represented by important commentators such as John of Rupescissa.[116]

While, as might be expected, the Franciscan impact on the laity was most marked in Italy and in southern France, which had close connections with the peninsula,[117] the Dominicans have been more closely associated with northern beguines.[118] Both orders fulfilled their mandate of supervising and channelling the spiritual aspirations of the laity and were especially concerned in finding for women, and with them, ways of expressing their devotion within the limits allowed to them. Both orders developed new avenues for women's spiritual yearnings.[119]

Douceline's total adherence to the Franciscan ideal cannot be completely ascribed to Hugh's influence, since both were raised in a family which practised the lessons of St. Francis on poverty and charity. St. Francis was a constant reference for her, present in all the major decisions she took, her supporter and protector, the guarantor of her community's permanence. Praying at his altar or reading his Life were occasions of ecstatic ravishment (9:42–44). Her special love for him, Christ's "keeper of the seal" (9:44), "Christ's standard-bearer" (9:43; 9:44; 10:36) could not be dissociated from her love for Christ himself and the Virgin.[120] Inspired by the model of St. Francis, Douceline was an integral part of the Franciscan movement and of its struggles in Provence. Without a proper church of their own, the ladies of Roubaud said their office and prayed in the church

---

116 On this fourteenth-century Franciscan Joachimite commentator, see Bignami-Odier. A revealing illustration of both is the apocalyptic nature of the visions received by Constance of Rabastens between 1384 and 1386, then transcribed by her confessor Raymond of Sabanac in her *Book of Revelations* (Hiver-Bérenguier).

117 We are told, for example, about St. Francis appealing "in lingua francigena" for help in building his church in Assisi (Brooke and Brooke, 278).

118 Without excluding the Dominican influence in Italy, as the figure of Catherine of Siena shows. McDonnell 126, 187, 203.

119 The emphasis put by Bell (84, 149), Vauchez (1981, 248–49 and 409; 1987a, 189–90) and Beckwith (212) on the attraction of Franciscanism for women must be qualified, notably according to Grundmann and also Neel's observations about the origins of the beguines in Premonstratensian and Cistercian ways of dealing with women seeking pious lives.

120 These ways of designating St. Francis betray the influence of the Franciscan preaching where the saint is seen as a prophet, a new Elijah, a latter-day herald of the final age which has an eschatological significance: Lerner (1974, 486–87) quotes a sermon of Bonaventure with St. Francis as Christ's arms bearer. We know that Bonaventure identified him with the angel of Revelation.

of the Friars Minor. It was there that Douceline had most of her ecstasies and levitations and where important people as well as ordinary folk came to contemplate her. She was well connected to major leaders of the order, to John of Parma, General Minister who supported her community, to Brother Jaucelin, provincial minister, later Bishop of Orange, who was her spiritual guide and friend after Hugh's death.

If St. Francis and the Friars Minor shaped Douceline's religious orientation and piety, she in return, through the authority conferred by her mystical experiences, was instrumental in the solution of tensions involving the Franciscan Order. We have seen how her intervention with the countess of Provence contributed to the safe delivery of a girl and then to a reconciliation between the Minors and the count.[121] More generally, we may suggest that the prestige of her sainthood helped in legitimizing the Spiritual orientation of the Franciscans which she and Hugh represented. In one of her visions at the altar of St. Francis in the church of the Friars, she prophesied that his views would be severely attacked but that he would "win the day and be victorious" (9:43). In fact, the systematic battle against the Spirituals began only at the turn of the century, at about the time when Philippine was composing her biography.

Two particular characteristics of her theology indicate Douceline's sympathy with the position of the Spirituals: her dedication to poverty and the Joachimite flavour of her devotion to St. Francis. We may find, in this orientation of her piety, another possible explanation of her unwillingness to join a regular order and her determination to maintain her own institution. Although the choice of poverty and the commitment to charitable work are the marks of the beguines' way of life, Douceline's motivation came mainly from her conformity to the model of St. Francis. We know that a major deciding factor was the vision she had of Christ in the guise of a poor, sick man asking for her compassion, a vision reminiscent of Christ's first appearance to Francis (1:7).[122] Francis's example prompted her solemn vow of poverty and the choice of her habit: as he adopted Christ's garments, she would wear those of the mourning Virgin (5:9). Her renunciation of possessions was uncompromising, for the community as well as for herself: she refused

---

121   The Franciscans were involved in the conflict with the count and the town of Marseilles because they sided with the town in the struggle for the recognition of its rights (Gout, 25).

122   Habig, 637.

donations made to her in particular by Philippine, and is shown resisting being blackmailed by a devotee who offered funds to her establishment in exchange for revelations he wanted from her (4:8). She only accepted alms in small amounts for giving them to the poor or putting them in the common purse (5:5; 5:8). Illustrating her extreme indifference to material goods, we are told that the sisters provided everything necessary for her and that she did not even have a robe or a bed sheet to be buried in (5:3–4).[123] The same rigour did not apply to her companions, to whom she preached moderation, nor to the institution; as uncloistered women they could keep their belongings and enjoy economic autonomy.[124] For the other members of the Roubaud community, Franciscan poverty was an inspiration that did not preclude possession of the material necessities required for its security.

The Joachimite trend within the Franciscan order had a most eloquent spokesman in Douceline's brother, Hugh. Salimbene, who was not himself a Joachimite devotee, was among the pious laymen who gathered around Hugh when he spoke on Joachim of Fiore and saw that he "had all the books, in elaborate versions" that the Abbot wrote.[125] He then recounts a debate between a Dominican brother and Hugh on the substance of Joachim's exegesis of the Apocalypse, a disputation won by the Franciscan, appropriate revenge on the Preachers who used to scorn the ignorance of the Friars.[126] We know also that the Joachimite sympathies of John of Parma, Douceline's spiritual mentor after Hugh's death, forced him to resign his position as Minister General.[127]

Despite the indisputable influence of both her brother and her

---

[123] We cannot agree with Carozzi 1975, 200, who considers that Douceline's Joachimism is central to her experience but not her dedication to poverty.

[124] We have seen that Philippine kept her wealth and could secure property for the community. For the attitude of the Belgian beguines toward poverty, see Little, 132–33.

[125] Salimbene 228. Reeves identifies the Joachimist influence on Franciscanism as early as 1221 in Calabria (1969, 38). See also Paul; Burr 1993, 3–5. Reeves (1961, 299) thinks, however, that Hugh reflects general trends of contemporary thought about Joachimism rather that being a real Joachimite himself.

[126] Salimbene, 231–46. St. Francis as the Angel of the Sixth Seal and the second Christ (Reeves 1969, 300–302; Burr 1985, 278, and Burr 1989a); the Spirituals considered themselves as the only "sealed" and therefore saved: Emmerson and Herzman, 31–39, 40–45. See also Rusconi for the diffusion of Joachimism among Franciscans.

[127] Burr 1993, 8–14.

mentor on her, the "apocalyptic imagination" is not prevalent in Douceline's theology.[128] Nevertheless, her Life is not without Joachimite allusions, such as the preaching about the imminent "terrible punishment" to be visited on the world (9:57) and about the empire to come (9:61).[129] Her visions of the Trinity guaranteeing and protecting her institution – which lead her to institute a daily devotion in "remembrance of the Holy Trinity" – might also have Joachimist undertones, given their allusion to the third state of history (10:21–25). In that Age of the Spirit, the *Ordo monachorum* will prevail, representing the accomplishment of spirituality, a prediction the two mendicant orders – especially the Spirituals – applied to themselves as the new spiritual men and women prophesied.[130] Some of her visions of the Virgin suggest the same inspiration. In the first one, Douceline is shown a crib with the Christ child among lilies, being fed by the Holy Spirit, an image reminiscent of the infant born to the Woman in the Apocalypse and nourished in the desert (10:11).[131] The other one, where the Virgin is sitting on the top of a hill surrounded by lilies, having being brought there by the Holy Spirit, evokes the third age of the Holy Spirit (10:12). If we consider that, when Philippine composed the Life and at the time when the second version was being prepared, non-authorized interpretations – in particular about the Trinity – were highly suspect in the eye of the Church, we may suppose that this aspect of Douceline's theology might well have been underplayed.

Douceline as the second Holy Mother

The most revealing element in Douceline's apocalyptic imagery is the place given to the figure of Christ's mother Mary who is, with St. Francis, the major inspiration of her spirituality. Yet both models should not be considered at the same level. Even if Francis may, in Joachimite representations, attain the status of second Christ, he remains a man who has achieved sainthood, something that she can accomplish herself by also leading a holy life. If Francis received the grace of being a second Christ through his deeds, why could she not aspire to become a second Mary? If the vita never makes such a bold proposition explicit, the elements are present for justifying the hypothesis. The parallel is drawn at several points in the text, as when

128 The expression is borrowed from Emmerson and Herzman.
129 Related to a quotation from Isaiah (1:5).
130 Reeves 1969, 18–19 and 142–48; Reeves 1980, 288–97; Burr 1983.
131 Apocalypse 12:1–6.

Douceline's choice of clothing and her vocation of suffering for "the love of the poor mother of Jesus Christ" are explained: "Just as Saint Francis had adopted the clothing of the Lord, she took those of the mother" (5:9). The most transparent allusion is the second of her apocalyptic visions. She was the only one to be allowed within the enclosure on top of the hill, surrounded by lilies, where the Queen, the mother of God, stayed alone and gave her many comforts and favours. The others who had been brought "in this glorious place" by the Holy Spirit had to stay outside of the enclosure to pray to the Virgin (10:12).

The imitation of Christ is the path prescribed to the pious woman in her progress toward sainthood, the goal which motivates her choice of a life of renouncement of earthly gratifications for the exclusive love of the crucified Christ (2:9). In this sense, Douceline conformed to the christocentrism predominant in beguine spirituality. She worked hard to eradicate any worldly affection in the sisters of the community, love of their parents included; their exclusive and complete dedication was to be to Jesus (6:7). Their vocation, as she instructed them, was to weep for Christ's sufferings, remembering his Passion every day in their prayers (3:7), a compassion she herself manifested without reserve (7:7; 9:49; 9:56). Although her love for Christ is described as so intense that "when she heard anything said about it, she would immediately be stirred and afire, so much so, that in her body and on her face, she showed outward signs of that flame that burned for the love of the Lord" (8:1), we fail to find the metaphors often used to designate the beguine's union with Christ. She is not described as the beloved or the spouse of the divine bridegroom,[132] but rather presented as his widow (3:7). Whereas Christ was at the centre of the Belgian beguines's piety, to the extent that Margaret of Ypres, for example, clung so much to Jesus that she could only think a little of his mother, Douceline's attention was mainly drawn to Mary.[133] The spiritual persona she adopted was not the loving bride who yearned for a mystical union with Christ but that of the caring mother and the afflicted widow, as symbolized by her habit with the mantle covering her head (2:9). Douceline, who is

---

[132] Lutgard of Aywières (Thomas de Cantimpré 1991, 36–37, 86); Margaret of Ypres (Thomas de Cantimpré 1996, 20–22); Yvette of Huy (Hugh of Floreffe, 47, 109); Marie d'Oignies (Jacques de Vitry, 42).

[133] Margaret of Ypres (Thomas de Cantimpré 1996, 46); Yvette of Huy had also a special interest in the Virgin who comforted her with the idea that it was impossible to serve one without serving the other (Hugh of Floreffe, 85).

constantly referred to as the "holy mother" (*la sancta maire*) in the vita, invests that role with a strong sense of her responsibility toward her "daughters" and the community she established for them.[134] Like a mother, she brings comfort to a 12-year old novice, putting her arms around her, her hand on her head, and addressing her as "my child" (11:15). This dual persona of widow and mother was one she had already learned to perform as a child after the death of her own mother, and was how she identified herself for both her worldly and her heavenly fathers.

The marks of Douceline's special link with the Virgin, a link which amounts to identification, are apparent throughout the vita from the first crucial moment of the encounter on the road near Hyères (1:3–7) until her funerals when the office of the Virgin was chanted (13:22; 14:20). We learn that Friar Jaucelin had been sent to her as her spiritual director after the death of her brother, by the Virgin herself who approved the special affection between them (10:3). Indeed, the Virgin provides counselling and comfort as a true beguine would (10:16), suggesting that the remark that "Our Lady was the first beguine" must be taken literally (2:11). The mother of Roubaud, for her part, acquires the status of an intercessor, caring for souls "as if they were her children in Christ" (7:3) so that she rightly deserves to be called Our Lady: "Nostra Donna". The cycle of identifications is extended by an image of Jesus as mother expressed in very explicit terms by Douceline's words of consolation to the sisters, grieving for her imminent loss: "Do you know that the Lord acts like a mother feeding her child?" (13:10). To this image one cannot help relating the dream of a pious countess "who saw an oil that was very pure and sweet and clear, like gold, flowing from the holy mother's [Douceline's] breast", an oil which was burning in a lamp in front of the altar of the Virgin (10:9).

Not surprisingly, Douceline's most significant visions and levitations occur precisely on the feast of the Assumption of the Virgin, on 15 August, in particular the last one before her death (9:12; 13:5–8). The details of these events deserve careful consideration because they present her levitations as a real emulation and re-enactment of the Virgin's assumption.

Douceline's spectacular manifestations, in Philippine's depiction of them, present strong parallels with the widely circulated text, *The Resurrection of the Blessed Virgin*, written by the German mystic,

---

[134] See Heffernan, 283, about the image of a mystic woman as a spiritual mother.

Elisabeth of Schönau, more than a century earlier. Describing her vision of the Virgin on 15 August 1157, Elisabeth wrote:

And I saw in a far-away place a tomb surrounded by great light, and what looked like the form of a woman in it, with a great multitude of angels standing around. After a little while, she was raised up from the tomb and, together with that multitude standing by, she was lifted up on high.[135]

Douceline's last levitation occurred just at the moment when the Vespers of the Virgin were being said:

And just when the officiant intoned the first antiphony that says "*Assumpta est Maria in celum, gaudent angeli*", she suddenly rose up into the air so high that it seemed as if she would keep on rising. (13:6)[136]

Philippine's voice

The main difference between the vitae of the northern beguines and this Life of Douceline is the fact that this narration was written not by a male spiritual partner but by a woman sharing the subject's experience from inside and, therefore, someone whose objectives are likely to be more closely identified with those of her subject. Philippine herself hints at the special relationship she developed with Douceline, telling how, having been attracted to the beguine's way of life by the sight of the enraptured mother, she had been assured that she was loved "among all the others" (11:12–14). Drawing general conclusions regarding the differences resulting from a feminine authorship is premature and could only be attempted after a thorough analysis of the few other surviving mystic biographies by female authors. In Philippine's case, our investigation of her narrative strategies will centre less on the consequences of gender than on the purpose of her enterprise of publicizing Douceline's achievement through a text written not in Latin, the clerical language, but in the vernacular.

We know that the purpose of Jacques de Vitry and Thomas de Cantimpré's biographies, in promoting the lives of holy women, was to persuade the ecclesiastical institution to recognize and legitimate their marginal forms of religiosity. Philippine, in presenting an Occitan demonstration of the founder of the Roubaud community's

---

135 Elisabeth of Schönau (Clark, 209–10). The vision was meant to demonstrate that Mary was taken up to heaven "in flesh as well as in spirit".
136 See also 9:69; 9:71; 9:73.

holiness does not aim at the same public. Her first and primary readership was intended to be the group of sisters whose prioress she had been even before Douceline's death. Following the death of the mother, Philippine bore the increased responsibility of maintaining the unity of the two houses of Hyères and Marseilles under circumstances which were becoming increasingly difficult because of attacks against the Spiritual fringe of the Franciscans and their lay followers.[137] One can wonder also if she did not find an additional need to reactivate the cult around Douceline, and hence an additional motivation for writing the Life, in 1297, the year of the death of another charismatic Franciscan saint, Louis of Anjou, himself identified with the Spiritual orientation and a follower of Olivi.[138] Philippine acts as the heir and continuator of Douceline's great *oeuvre* in producing this textual monument to her glory; in doing so, she establishes her presence for ever. The complementarity of both women and the coincidence of their goals is such that the question of Philippine's own voice can be raised. Is it possible to find her behind the carefully constructed image she presents of a saintly life? Does she remain totally hidden behind the icon she is building? In other words, what are her narrative strategies for allowing us to differentiate between Douceline's mission and hers?

We will see how these strategies are related to Philippine's main preoccupation as it appears in her text: the question of validating a way of life and a form of dedication which stands at the margins of what is acceptable for the ecclesiastical institution. Douceline's experience and status of sainthood has to be authenticated first because it legitimizes what is also promoted by the vita, the Roubaud community and the biography itself; all three aspects are tightly interconnected. Conforming herself to the usual practice of the "hagiobiographer" of appealing to the evidence of reliable witnesses, Philippine is not satisfied with the general statement that many people "bore true testimony" of the truth of the saint's raptures and miracles. Most of the time, she provides names, choosing as trust-

---

[137] One is tempted to take at face value, and in their literal sense, the words the "blows" and the "trials" which are anticipated, and to appreciate, in the context of inquisitorial investigation, her faith in God's assistance in responding to "all the questions" that they could encounter (14:33).
[138] Vauchez 1981, 265–66. His body was also placed with those of Hugh and Douceline in the church of the Franciscans in Marseilles. The year 1297 is also the date of the nomination of a new provincial minister, Arnaud de Roquefeuil, who was hostile to the Spirituals and attacked Olivi and his followers (Peano, 51).

worthy guarantors members of the nobility like lady Beatrice or Huguette de Fos, the wife of the lord of the castle in Hyères (9:8; 9:12; 9:73).[139] The same need to authenticate Douceline's ecstatic experiences explains the many mentions of witnesses measuring the distance between the ground and her feet as well as the most questionable practice of harming her as a test. The procedures culminate with Philippine's last statements where she intervenes in her own voice in a strikingly formal tone, attesting to the quality of her work: "We swear that what we have put in writing is told truthfully. We have left out many other miracles that we learned about from the people involved but did not write down because we did not have reliable or sworn testimony" (15:43).[140]

Her other personal intervention, shifting from the third person of the biographer and prioress of the community to the first person, occurs in chapter 14, precisely after she has recounted a series of events meant simultaneously to support Douceline's sainthood and the legitimacy of the community, and hence the validity of the biography (14:31–33). We find in this passage of the vita a summary of its purpose: that the order founded by Douceline as well as the sisters themselves, are under the protection of the Lord. This protected status is enjoyed for three reasons: the guarantee of St. Francis, the instruction of Hugh's doctrine, and the example provided by the "holy mother".

A second shift, characteristic of the sections of the biography which relate to these concerns of its author, transforms her into a gifted storyteller, the narrator indulging in a precise account of all the details surrounding the facts, in a striking contrast with the succinctness of the rest of the vita. The first of these lengthy episodes, culminating with the assurance made to the sisters that their house is blessed, develops like a staged drama where Douceline, followed by the sisters, walks in rapture in the dormitory, singing in a sweet and languid way, using words they could not distinctly understand (9:59–64).[141] But Philippine's narrative strategy is mostly remarkable in chapter 14 which deals with Douceline's afterlife, and reads like a short story, beginning with

---

139 In some cases, the mention of numbers of people observing the levitation and measuring it also supplies the identification of the witness.

140 She managed to get one of these sworn testimonies from the mother of Pellegrin, the crippled boy she cured and who became a Franciscan (12:22).

141 This pentecostal kind of "speaking in tongues" happens at the eve of the Ascension.

disagreements in the convent at Marseilles about the sanctity of the mother of Roubaud, disagreements occurring precisely at the time when her Life was written (14:6–23). The narrative continues with the details of Douceline's apparition to a novice, sick in bed because of her anxiety about the conflict, and the cure she performed on her, then proceeds to the vision of the saint experienced during the celebration of the matins, in a precisely staged dramaturgy. Another episode, of a vision experienced by a sister, confirming the sanctity of their institution, is cleverly rendered with a dialogue between Jesus Christ and the saints who inquire about this order which is unknown to them.

The stylistic contrast between the sections which deal directly with issues concerning the community and the rest of the biography can be attributed to Philippine's specific interest in them. They transcend, however, the conscious display of her narrative talents, in that they convey, in a particularly clear way, a representation of the mystical exchange with God, based on the notion that the body itself is the vehicle and the sign of this communication. The few words which are reported from Douceline's ecstatic experiences are bursts of pain or joy, closer to a cry or to music than to articulated language (9:49; 9:57; 9:61–69; 14:25–26). Her experience manifests in an exemplary fashion this conception of sainthood as an energy flowing into the saint's body, illuminating and transforming her face which is usually ravaged by mortification. This idea that the body becomes totally transparent and no longer an obstacle extends to her daughters during Douceline's apparition to them: their joyful bliss showed on their faces as "a sign of the glory they were feeling in their souls" (14:18). A revealing touch confirming her holiness is the mention of the "celestial fragrance" surrounding her, a typical "proof" which has become a cliché of so many saints' lives (14:17).[142] This special odour confirms indeed that the efforts invested in mastering the flesh in all its worldly needs have been successful in transforming the body into pure spirit. The transmutation is expressed in the form of an oxymoronic opposition between the aesthete's declining body and her growing energy and enthusiasm (13:2). In Douceline's case, however, determination and fortitude are also attributes characterizing her personality and defining her identity. Philippine compares her resoluteness to a cornerstone or a column and describes how,

---

[142] Vauchez 1981, 500. A typical characteristic also is the observation concerning beauty (15:6).

even if "afflicted by a great deal of physical suffering", "she held herself upright" when reciting the hours (10:4–7). Strength and determination were indeed as much needed from the founder and leader of the community as the tenderness of the mother. And yet it is the sweet Douceline that Philippine wants her audience to remember, putting her arms around a 12-year-old novice (11:15), weeping as she touches a severely diseased and deformed child (12:12–16) passing "her hand gently" over the feet of a sick sister (14:10), and humbly washing the feet of her ladies of Roubaud (12:8).

Bibliography

Albanés, J.H. (1879). *La Vie de Sainte Douceline fondatrice des béguines de Marseille*. Marseille: Camoin.

Aurill, Martin (1986). *Une Famille de la noblesse provençale au moyen âge: les Porcelet*. Aubanel: Archives du Sud.

Baird, Joseph L., Giuseppe Baglivi and John Robert Kane (1986). *The Chronicle of Salimbene de Adam*. Binghamton: Medieval and Renaissance Texts and Studies.

Baratier, Édouard (1973a). "Le mouvement mendiant à Marseille". In *Les Mendiants en pays d'oc au XIIIe siècle. Cahiers de Fanjeaux* 8. Toulouse: Privat, 177–91.

—— (1973b). *Histoire de Marseille*. Toulouse: Privat.

Barone, Giulia (1992). "L'oeuvre eschatologique de Pierre Jean-Olieu et son influence. Un bilan historiographique". In *Fin du monde et signes des temps. Visionnaires et prophètes en France Méridionale (fin XIIIe–début XVe siècle). Cahiers de Fanjeaux* 27. Toulouse: Privat, 49–61.

Beatrice of Nazareth, see De Ganck.

Beckwith, Sarah (1996). "A Very Material Mysticism: The Medieval Mysticism of Margery Kempe". In Chance, 195–215.

Bell, Rudolph M. (1985). *Holy Anorexia*. Chicago: University of Chicago Press.

Bériou, Nicole (1990). "Saint François, premier prophète de son ordre, dans les sermons du XIIIe siècle". *Mélanges de l'École Française de Rome: Moyen Âge* 102/2, 535–56.

—— (1998). "The Right of Women to Give Religious Instruction in the Thirteenth Century". In *Women Preachers and Prophets Through Two Millennia of Christianity*. Ed. Beverly Mayne Kienzle and Pamela J. Walker. Berkeley: University of California Press, 134–45.

Bignami-Odier, Jeanne (1952). *Etudes sur Jean de Roquetaillade (Johannes de Rupescissa)*. Paris: Vrin.

Birgitta, see Gregersson.

Blumenfeld-Kosinski, Renate, and Timea Szell (eds) (1991). *Images of Sainthood in Medieval Europe*. Ithaca and London: Cornell University Press.

Bolton, Brenda (1976). "*Mulieres Sanctae*". In *Women in Medieval*

Society. Ed. Susan Mosher Stuard, Philadelphia: University of Pennsylvania Press, 141–58.

————— (1978). "*Vitae Matrum*: A Further Aspect of the *Frauenfrage*". In *Medieval Women*. Ed. Derek Baker. Oxford: Basil Blackwell, 253–73.

Boureau, Alain (1994). "The Sacrality of one's own Body in the Middle Ages". *Yale French Studies* 86, 5–17.

Brooke, Rosalind B., and Christopher N.L. Brooke (1978). "St. Clare". In *Medieval Women*. Ed. Derek Baker. Oxford: Basil Blackwell, 275–87.

Brunel-Lobrichon, Geneviève (1988a). "Existe-t-il un christianisme méridional? L'exemple de Douceline: le béguinage provençal". *Hérésies* 11, 41–51.

————— (1988b). "Diffusion et spiritualité des premières clarisses méridionales". *Cahiers de Fanjeaux* 23. Toulouse: Privat, 261–80.

————— (1997). "Légendes de saint François en langues romanes". In *Francescanesimo in volgare (secoli XIII–XIV). Atti del XXIV Convegno internazionale, Assisi, 17–19 ottobre 1996*. Spoleto: Centro italiano di studi sull'alto medioevo, 161–78.

Burr, David (1983). "Bonaventure, Olivi and Franciscan Eschatology". *Collectanea Franciscana* 53, 23–40.

————— (1985). "Olivi, Apocalyptic Expectation, and Visionary Experience". *Traditio* 41, 273–288.

————— (1989a). "Franciscan Exegesis and Francis as Apocalyptic Figure", In *Monks, Nuns, and Friars in Medieval Society*. Ed. Edward B. King, Jacqueline T. Schaefer and William B. Wadley. Sewanee, Tennessee: The Press of the University of the South, 51–62.

————— (1989b). *Olivi and Franciscan Poverty: The Origins of the "Usus Pauper" Controversy*. Philadelphia: University of Pennsylvania Press.

————— (1993). *Olivi's Peaceable Kingdom: A Reading of The Apocalypse Commentary*. Philadelphia: University of Pennsylvania Press.

Bynum, Caroline Walker (1982). *Jesus as Mother: Studies in the Spirituality of the High Middle Ages*. Berkeley: University of California Press.

————— (1986). " 'And Woman His Humanity': Female Imagery in the Religious Writing of the Later Middle Ages". In *Gender and Religion: On the Complexity of Symbols*. Ed. Caroline Walker Bynum, Stevan Harrell and Paula Richman. Boston: Beacon Press, 257–88.

————— (1987). *Holy Feast and Holy Fast: The Religious Significance of Food to Medieval Women*. Berkeley: University of California Press.

—— (1991). *Fragmentation and Redemption: Essays on Gender and the Human Body in Medieval Religion*. New York: Zone Books.

Cambell, Jacques (1963). *Vies Occitanes de Saint Auzias et de Sainte Dauphine*. Rome: Pontificium Athenaeum Antonianum.

Camille, Michael (1994). "The Image and the Self: Unwriting Late Medieval Bodies". In Kay and Rubin, 62–99.

Carozzi, Claude (1973). "L'*estamen* de sainte Douceline". *Provence historique* 23, fasc. 93–94, 270–79.

—— (1975). "Une Béguine Joachimite: Douceline, Soeur d'Hugues de Digne". In *Franciscains d'oc. Les Spirituels, ca. 1280–1324. Cahiers de Fanjeaux* 10. Toulouse: Privat, 169–201.

—— (1976). "Douceline et les autres". In *La religion populaire en Languedoc du XIIIe siècle à la moitié du XIVe siècle. Cahiers de Fanjeaux* 11. Toulouse: Privat, 251–267.

Chance, Jane (1996). *Gender and Text in the Later Middle Ages*. Gainsville: University Press of Florida.

Christina the Astonishing, see Thomas de Cantimpré.

Clark, Anne L. (ed.) (2000). *Elisabeth of Schönau: The Complete Works*. New York: Paulist Press.

Coakley, John (1991a). "Friars as Confidants of Holy Women in Medieval Dominican Hagiography". In Blumenfeld-Kosinski and Szell, 222–46.

—— (1991b). Gender and the Authority of Friars: the Significance of Holy Women for Thirteenth-Century Franciscans and Dominicans". *Church History* 60, 445–60.

Congar, Yves M.-J. (1961–62). "Aspects ecclésiologiques de la querelle entre mendiants et séculiers dans la seconde moitié du XIIIe siècle et le début du XIVe siècle". *Archives d'histoire doctrinale et littéraire du Moyen âge* 36, 35–151.

Constable, Giles (1996). "Attitudes Towards Self-inflicted Suffering in Middle Ages". In *Culture and Spirituality in the Medieval Europe*. Brookfield: Collected Studies Series, Variorum, 7–27.

Daniel, E. Randolph (1975). "A Re-Examination of the Origins of Franciscan Joachimism". In *Joachim of Fiore in Christian Thought: Essays on the Influence of the Calabrian Prophet*. Ed. Delno C. West. New York: Burt Franklin, 143–48.

Dauphine de Puimichel, see Cambell.

De Ganck, Roger (1991). *The Life of Beatrice of Nazareth, 1200–1280*. Kalamazoo, MI: Cistercian Publications.

Dossat, Yves (1967). "Les Vaudois méridionaux d'après les documents de l'Inquisition". In *Vaudois et Pauvres catholiques. Cahiers de Fanjeaux* 2. Toulouse: Privat, 207–26.

Durieux, François-Régis (1973). "Approches de l'histoire franciscaine du Languedoc au XIIIe siècle". In *Les Mendiants en pays d'oc. Cahiers de Fanjeaux* 8. Toulouse: Privat, 79–100.

Elisabeth of Schönau, see Clark.

Emmerson, Richard K., and Ronald B. Herzman (1992). *The Apocalyptic Imagination in Medieval Literature*. Philadelphia: University of Pennsylvania Press.

Finke, Laurie A. (1992), "The Grotesque Mystical Body: Representing the Woman Writer". In *Feminist Theory: Women's Writing*. Ithaca and London: Cornell University Press, 75–107.

——— (1993). "Mystical Bodies and the Dialogics of Vision". In Wiethaus 1993, 28–44.

Galloway, Penelope (1997). "*Discreet and Devout Maidens*: Women's Involvement in Beguine Communities in Northern France, 1200–1500". In *Medieval Women in their Communities*. Ed. Diane Watt. Toronto: University of Toronto Press, 92–115.

Geary, Patrick J. (1978). *Furta Sacra: Thefts of Relics in the Central Middle Ages*. Princeton: Princeton University Press.

——— (1986). "Sacred Commodities: The Circulation of Medieval Relics". In *The Social Life of Things: Commodities in Cultural Perspective*. Ed. Arjun Appadurai. Cambridge: Cambridge University Press, 169–91.

Gilchrist, Roberta (1994). "Medieval Bodies in the Material World: Gender, Stigma and the Body". In Kay and Rubin, 43–61.

Goodich, Michael (1982). *Vita Perfecta: The Ideal of Sainthood in the Thirteenth Century*. Stuttgart: Anton Hiersemann.

Gout, R. (1927). *La Vie de Sainte Douceline. Texte provençal du XIVe siècle. Traduction et notes par R. Gout (Vida de la Benhaurada Sancta Douceline)*. Paris: Librairie Bloud et Gay.

Greenspan, Kate (1996). "Autohagiography and Medieval Women's Spiritual Autobiography". In Chance, 216–36.

Gregersson, Birger, and Thomas Gascoigne (1991). *The Life of Saint Birgitta*. Trans. Julia Bolton Holloway. Toronto: Peregrina.

Grundmann, Herbert (1995). *Religious Movements in the Middle Ages*. Trans. Steven Rowan. Notre Dame, IN: University of Notre Dame Press.

Habig, Marion A. (ed. and trans.) (1973). *St. Francis of Assisi: Writings and Early Biographies*. London: SPCK.

Haskins, Susan (1993). *Mary Magdalen: Myth and Metaphor*. London: HarperCollins.

Heffernan, Thomas J. (1988). *Sacred Biography: Saints and their Biog-*

raphers in the Middle Ages. New York and Oxford: Oxford University Press.

Hiver-Bérenguier, Jean-Pierre (1984). *Constance de Rabastens. Mystique de Dieu ou de Gaston Fébus?* Toulouse: Privat.

Hugh of Floreffe (1999). *"The Life of Yvette of Huy".* Trans. Jo Ann McNamara. Toronto: Peregrina.

Jacques de Vitry (1998). *The Life of Marie d'Oignies.* Trans. Margot H. King. Toronto: Peregrina.

Joinville (1998). *Vie de Saint Louis.* Ed. Jacques Monfrin. Paris: Garnier.

Juliana of Mont-Cornillon, see Newman (1999).

Kay, Sarah, and Miri Rubin (eds) (1994). *Framing Medieval Bodies.* Manchester and New York: Manchester University Press.

Kienzle, Beverly Mayne, and Pamela J. Walker (eds) (1998). *Women Preachers and Prophets Through Two Millennia of Christianity.* Berkeley: University of California Press.

Lambert, Malcolm David (1961). *Franciscan Poverty: The Doctrine of the Absolute Poverty of Christ and the Apostles in the Franciscan Order, 1210–1323.* London: SPCK.

Lauwers, Michel (1989). "Expérience béguinale et récit hagiographique. A propos de la *Vita Mariae Oigniacencis* de Jacques de Vitry (vers 1215)". *Journal des Savants,* Janvier, 61–103.

Le Goff, Jacques (1984). *The Birth of Purgatory.* Chicago: University of Chicago Press.

Lerner, Robert E. (1974). "A Collection of Sermons Given in Paris c. 1267, Including a New Text by Saint Bonaventura on the Life of Saint Francis". *Speculum* 49, 466–98.

———— (1992). "Ecstatic Dissent". *Speculum* 67, 33–57.

Little, Lester K. (1978). *Religious Poverty and the Profit Economy in Medieval Europe.* Ithaca: Cornell University Press.

Ludwig-Jansen, Katherine (1998). "Maria Magdalena: Apostolorum Apostola". In Kienzle and Walker, 57–96.

———— (2000). *The Making of the Magdalen: Preaching and Popular Devotion in the Later Middle Ages.* Princeton: Princeton University Press.

Lutgard of Aywières, see Thomas de Cantimpré.

Mahoney, Dhira B. (1992), "Margery Kempe's Tears and the Power over Language". In *Margery Kempe: A Book of Essays.* Ed. Sandra J. McEntire. New York and London: Garland, 37–50.

Manselli, Raoul (1976). "Les opuscules spirituels de Pierre-Jean Olivi et la piété des béguins de Langue d'oc". In *La Religion Populaire en*

Languedoc du XIIIe à la moitié du XIVe siècle. Cahiers de Fanjeaux 11. Toulouse: Privat, 187–201.

—— (1989). *Spirituels et béguins du Midi*, Toulouse: Privat.

Marie d'Oignies, see Jacques de Vitry.

Margaret of Ypres, see Thomas de Cantimpré.

McDonnell, E.W. (1954). *The Beguines and Beghards in Medieval Culture with Special Emphasis on the Belgian Scene.* New Jersey: Rutgers University Press (repr. New York, 1969).

McGinn, Bernard (1979). *Visions of the End: Apocalyptic Traditions in the Middle Ages.* New York: Columbia University Press.

McGuire, Brian Patrick (1989). "Purgatory, the Communion of Saints, and Medieval Change". *Viator* 20, 61–84.

McNamara, Jo Ann (1991). "The Need to Give: Suffering and Female Sanctity in the Middle Ages". In Blumenfeld-Kosinski and Szell, 199–221.

—— (1993). "The Rhetoric of Orthodoxy: Clerical Authority and Female Innovation in the Struggle with Heresy". In Wiethaus 1993, 9–27.

Mollat, Michel (1978). *The Poor in the Middle Ages: An Essay in Social History.* New Haven: Yale University Press.

Moorman, Y. (1968). *A History of the Franciscan Order from its Origins to the Year 1517.* Oxford: Clarendon Press.

Muessig, Carolyn (1996). "Paradigms of Sanctity for Thirteenth-Century Women". In *Models of Holiness in Medieval Sermons.* Ed. Beverley Mayne Kienzle. Louvain-la Neuve: Fédération Internationale des Instituts d'Études Médiévales, 85–102.

—— (1998). "Prophecy and Song: Teaching and Preaching by Medieval Women". In Kienzle and Walker. 146–58.

Murk-Jansen, Saskia (1996). "The Use of Gender and Gender-Related Imagery in Hadewijch". In Chance, 52–68.

—— (1998). *Brides in the Desert: The Spirituality of the Beguines.* London: Darton, Longman & Todd.

Neel, Carol (1989). "The Origins of the Beguines". In *Sisters and Workers in the Middle Ages.* Ed. Judith M. Bennett. Chicago and London: Chicago University Press, 240–60.

Newman, Barbara (1991). *The Life of Juliana of Mont-Cornillon.* Toronto: Peregrina Translations Series, 3rd printing 1999.

—— (1995). *From Virile Woman to Woman Christ: Studies in Medieval Religion and Literature.* Philadelphia: University of Pennsylvania Press.

—— (1998). "Possessed by the Spirit: Devout Women, Demoniacs, and the Apostolic Life in the Thirteenth Century. *Speculum* 73, 733–70.

Paul, Jacques (1975). "Hugues de Digne". In *Franciscains d'oc. Les Spirituels ca. 1280–1324. Cahiers de Fanjeaux* 10. Toulouse: Privat, 69–97.

Peano, Pierre (1975). "Ministres provinciaux de Provence et Spirituels". In *Franciscains d'oc. Les Spirituels ca. 1280–1324. Cahiers de Fanjeaux* 10. Toulouse: Privat, 41–65.

Reeves, Marjory (1961). "Joachimist Influences on the Idea of a Last World Emperor". *Traditio* 17, 323–70.

——— (1969). *The Influence of Prophecy in the Later Middle Ages.* Oxford: Oxford University Press.

Roisin, Simone (1943). "L'efflorescence cistercienne et le courant féminin de piété au XIIIe siècle". *Revue d'histoire Ecclésiastique* 39, 342–79.

——— (1947). *L'hagiographie cistercienne dans le diocèse de Liége au XIIIe siècle.* Louvain and Brussels: Université de Louvain.

Rosenwein, Barbara M., and Lester K. Little (1974). "Social Meaning in the Monastic and Mendicant Spiritualities". *Past and Present* 63, 4–32.

Ross, Ellen (1993). " 'She Wept and Cried Right Loud for Sorrow and for Pain': Suffering, the Spiritual Journey, and Women's Experience in Late Medieval Mystics". In Wiethaus 1993, 45–59.

Runciman, Steven (1958). *The Sicilian Vespers: A History of the Mediterranean World in the Later Thirteenth Century.* Cambridge: Cambridge University Press (repr. Penguin Books, 1961).

Rusconi, Roberto (1992). "À la recherche des traces authentiques de Joachim de Flore dans la France méridionale". In *Fin du monde et signes des temps. Visionnaires et prophètes en France méridionale (fin XIIIe–début XVe siècle), Cahiers de Fanjeaux* 27. Toulouse: Privat, 63–80.

Salimbene de Adam, see Baird *et al.*

Saxer, Victor (1959). *Le culte de Marie Madeleine en Occident des origines à la fin du Moyen Âge.* Auxerre and Paris: Publications de la Société des Fouilles Archéologiques et des Monuments Historiques de l'Yonne-Librairie Chavreuil.

Schmidt, Margot, and Leonard P. Hindsley (eds) (1993). "Introduction" to *Margaret Ebner: Major Works.* New York: Paulist Press.

Schmitt, Jean-Claude (1978). *Mort d'une hérésie. L'Église et les clercs face aux béguines et aux béghards du Rhin supérieur du XIVe au XVe siècle.* Paris-La Haye: Mouton.

Simons, Walter (1994). "Reading a Saint's Body: Rapture and Bodily

Movement in the *Vitae* of Thirteenth-Century Beguines". In Kay and Rubin, 10–23.

————— and Joanna Ziegler (1990). "Phenomenal Religion in the Thirteenth Century and its Image: Elisabeth of Spalbeek and the Passion Cult". *Studies in Church History* 27, 117–35.

Sisto, Alessandra (1971). *Figure del Primo Francescanesimo in Provenza, Ugo e Douceline di Digne*. Milan: Leo S. Olschki.

Sweetman, Robert S. (1997). "Thomas of Cantimpré. *Mulieres Religiosae* and Purgatorial Piety: Hagiographical *Vitae* and the 'Beguine Voice' ". In *A Distinct Voice: Medieval Studies in Honor of Leonard Boyle O.P.* Ed. Jacqueline Brown and William P. Stoneman. Notre Dame: University of Notre Dame Press, 606–28.

Thomas de Cantimpré (1991). *The Life of Lutgard of Aywières*. Trans. Margot H. King. Toronto: Peregrina.

————— (1996). *The Life of Margaret of Ypres*. Trans. Margot H. King. Toronto: Peregrina.

————— (1999a). *The Supplement to Jacques de Vitry's "Life of Marie d'Oignies"*. Trans. Margot H. King. Toronto: Peregrina, 213–55.

————— (1999b). *The Life of Christina the Astonishing*. Trans. Margot H. King. Toronto: Peregrina.

Tibbets Schulenburg, Jane (1986). "The Heroics of Virginity: Brides of Christ and Sacrificial Mutilation". In *Women in the Middle Ages and the Renaissance*. Ed. Mary Beth Rose. Syracuse: Syracuse University Press, 29–72.

Vauchez, André (1981). *La sainteté en Occident aux derniers siècles du Moyen Âge d'après les procès de canonisation et les documents hagiographiques*. Rome: École Française de Rome.

————— (1987a). "La sainteté féminine dans le mouvement franciscain". In *Les laïcs au Moyen Âge. Pratiques et expériences religieuses*, Paris: Cerf, 189–209.

————— (1987b). "Prosélytisme et action antihérétique en milieu féminin au XIIIe siècle: la *Vie de Marie d'Oignies* (+1213) par Jacques de Vitry". In *Propagande et contre-propagande religieuses*. Ed. Jacques Marx. Brussels: Éditions de l'Université de Bruxelles, 95–110.

————— (1991). "Lay People's Sanctity in Western Europe: Evolution of a Pattern (Twelfth and Thirteenth Centuries)". In Blumenfeld-Kosinski and Szell, 21–32.

Wiethaus, Ulrike (1991). "Sexuality, Gender, and the Body in Late Medieval Women's Spirituality: Cases from Germany and the Netherlands". *Journal of Feminist Studies in Religion* 7, 35–52.

———— (ed.) (1993). *Maps of Flesh and Light: Religious Experience of Medieval Women Mystics.* Syracuse: Syracuse University Press.

Windeatt, B.A. (ed.) (1985). *The Book of Margery Kempe.* London: Penguin.

Yvette of Huy, see Hugh of Floreffe.

Ziegler, Joanna (1992). *Sculpture of Compassion: The Pietà and the Beguines in the Southern Low Countries, c.1300–1600.* Brussels: Institut Historique Belge de Rome.

———— (1993). "Reality as Imitation: The Dynamics of Imagery among the Beguines". In Wiethaus 1993, 112–26.

Index

Page number references are given except for references to the vita itself, where chapter and section references are provided in **bold** typeface.

abstinence, **6:3**, 121 and n, 124; see also anorexia, asceticism, fasting

Advent, **10:8**

Aix, 12n, **16:28**

Alaiette Martin, **15:18**

Albigensian heretics, 6, 7; see also Cathars

alms, **2:1, 5:5, 5:7–8, 5:11**, 151

angels, **3:9, 9:3, 9:24, 9:68–69, 9:74–75, 10:5, 10:11, 10:21, 13:6, 13:8, 14:17, 14:19**, 128, 129n, 131, 149n

Annunciation, feast of, 136

anorexia, 118, 128n, 138; see also abstinence, asceticism, fasting

Antioch, 8n, **7:4** and n, 122

apocalypse, 148, 151–53

appearances (of Douceline), 17, **4:11, 10:9, 13:23, 14:9–17, 14:20–21, 14:23, 14:25–27, 15:6–7, 15:13, 15:25, 15:27**, 130, 132, 135, 137, 141, 158; see also visions

Aragon, King of, **11:9**

Arnaud – see Nicolette

Arnaud de Roquefeuil, 156n

Artois, Count of, **9:36–40**, 131

Ascension, feast of, **9:59**, 138, 157n

asceticism, **6:2–3, 6:12, 16:6**, 115–16, 117 and n, 118, 120–21, 125–26, 127 and n, 128, 130, 141, 153; see also abstinence, anorexia, fasting

Assisi, 147, 149n

Assumption of the Virgin, feast of, **9:69–70, 9:73–74**, 65n, **9:69–70, 9:73–74, 13:5–6**, 89n, 131, 154

Augustine's *City of God*, 120

authorship, 15–18, 20, 135, 141, 155–58; see also Philippine

Auzias de Sabran, 18n

awls, **9:14–15**

Barjols, 7, **1:1, 1:3**

Barthélemy Martin, **15:16**

Beatrice (sister of Roubaud), **9:12**

Beatrice of Anjou, Countess of Provence, 8 and n, 11, **4:10–13, 9:33–34**, 132, 136, 150

Beatrice of Nazareth, 5n, 88n

beghards, 2, 9n, 13

beguins, 13 and n

beguinage, 3–7, 9, 13

beguine, 1–2, 4–6 and n, 8, 9 and n, 10n, 11–17, 18 and n, 19n, 21, **2:2, 2:11, 3:1, 3:8, 4:2, 4:11, 6:1, 12:8**, 91n, **14:12, 15:6, 15:13–14, 15:16, 15:22, 16:31**, 114n, 117, 119n, 121, 122n, 123, 125 and n, 126, 134, 140–42 145–48, 150, 153–56

beguine mysticism, 119, 153

Beguine heresy, 10; see also Free Spirit

Belgium (holy women in), 1, 5, 6 and n, 18 and n, 116–17, 119–28, 122n, 124n, 132–33, 138n, 142–43, 146–47, 149–50, 151n, 153; see also Flanders

Bérenguier (Douceline's father), 7, **1:1, 2:1**, 143

Bernard Gui, 10, 13, 148

birds, 21, **7:1–2, 13:4, 9:19**, 130, 133, 136

Birgitta of Sweden, 117n, 119n, 122n, 124n

blood, **7:3, 9:58, 9:66, 10:15**, 129

bodily needs, 115

body, **1:10–11, 1:13, 6:3, 6:8, 9:20–21, 9:28, 9:31, 9:35, 9:69, 9:43, 9:50, 9:66**, 89n, **15:3, 15:16**, 115–16, 118, 119 and n, 120 and n, 121, 122 and n, 123 and n, 124–27, 128 and n, 129, 136, 137 and n, 138, 139 and n, 158; D's body: **5:4, 6:13, 8:1,**

9:12, 9:14, 9:49, 9:69, 10:1, 10:15, 13:1–2, 13:6, 13:10, 153; body as corpse: **13:16–22, 14:1, 14:3, 14:5, 14:34–35**, 139, 147–48, 156n.
Bohemia, 9n
Bretheren of the Sack (Franciscans), 144–45
Burgundy, 15

calf, **9:54**, 125
canonization, 14, 17, 18n
Carpenella (sister of Cecilia), **15:9**
Cathars, 9, 120 and n; see also Albigensians
Catherine of Alexandria, 2n
Catherine of Siena, 149n
Cécile de la Voute, 15
Cecilia (of Marseilles), **15:8**
charity, 5, 8, 10, 19n, **1:1, 1:5, 1:6, 2:1, 2:10, 3:10, 5:1, 5:11–12, 7:8, 8:3–4, 8:6–7, 16:19, 16:32**, 125 and n, 129, 143, 149
charity (of Douceline), 7, **1:5, 1:7, 1:8, 2:1, 2:2, 3:10, 5:5, 6:8, 8:4–8, 8:10, 16:11, 16:13, 16:19**, 117, 122, 141–42, 147, 150–51
Charles I of Anjou, Count of Provence, King of Sicily, 8 and n, 11, 16–17, **4:10–14, 5:8, 9:16, 9:33, 9:38, 11:4–9**, 77n, 79n, 132 and n, 143, 150 and n
Charles II of Anjou, Count of Salerno, **11:9**, 79n
chastity, 3, 4, 9, 10 and n, 28n, **2:10, 16:21**, 118, 119; see also sexuality, and n, 142, 146
Christ, 19 and n, 22, **1:2, 2:9–10, 5:1–3, 5:9, 6:2, 6:4, 6:7, 7:1–3, 7:7, 8:4–6, 9:4–5, 9:43–44, 9:49, 9:55–56, 9:59**, 63n, **9:73, 10:4, 10:13, 10:15, 10:25, 10:29, 11:1, 12:15**, 92n, **13:22, 14:1, 14:3, 14:30–31, 14:34, 16:22, 16:33**, 117–18, 119n, 121n, 124–25, 127, 129n, 130 and n, 136, 138, 141, 142n, 145, 147, 149 and n, 150, 151n, 153–54, 158; Christ child, Nativity: **9:46, 9:67, 10:10–11**, 129, 152; Christ (bridegroom): 116n, 119n, 127, 153; see also Passion of Christ
Christ (appearances to Douceline), **1:6, 8:6–9, 10:15**, 129
Christina the Astonishing (of Saint-Trond), 7, 18, 19 and n, 122n, 123 and n, 124n, 126 and n, 127 and n, 132n, 133 and n, 134n, 146
Christmas, feast of, **9:45–46, 9:67, 10:10**, 131
Christocentrism, 122n, 153
Christopher of Cahors, 12n
Cistercians, 1, 3 and n, 120, 149n
Clare of Assisi, 4n, 120n
Cologne, 6n, 9n
Communion (sacrament), 20n, **9:7, 9:9, 9:12, 9:22, 9:24, 9:26–28, 9:33, 9:43, 9:46, 9:67, 9:69, 9:71, 10:13–15, 13:5**, 121, 125, 130; see also host (Eucharist)
community (Douceline's), 10, 12, 13, 15, 16, 21, **6:11, 9:12, 10:2, 11:12, 11:15, 11:18, 12:4, 12:6, 12:8, 13:11, 13:12, 13:15, 14:6, 14:23–24, 14:26–27, 15:9, 15:14, 15:15, 15:22, 15:24, 16:1, 16:23, 16:33**, 114n, 122, 126, 129, 131n, 134–35,151 and n, 152–56, 158–59; as institution: 6–8, 11, 17, 20–22, **2:7–8, 3:4–6, 4:1–2, 4:4**, 146; survival of the community: 10, 17, **3:6, 9:1, 9:64, 10:16–18, 10:20–25, 10:30–37, 14:28–33**, 116, 130–31, 138–41, 144–45, 147, 149–50, 156; see also Roubaud house
compassion, **1:1, 2:1, 5:6, 7:1, 7:6–8, 8:4, 8:6, 9:49, 12:2–3, 12:8, 12:13, 12:16, 12:23, 15:23, 15:25, 16:13**, 122, 124, 125, 150, 153; compassion for animals: **7:1–2, 12:3**
confession, **6:6, 9:11**
confessor, 6, 18, **10:3–4, 10:6, 10:15, 10:21, 15:35**, 123, 133n
Constance de Rabastens, 13, 130n, 149n
Constance of Cabriès, **15:2**
contemplation, **1:3, 9:3–4, 9:18, 9:45, 9:52, 10:10, 10:26, 11:2–3, 13:3, 16:16**, 124
convent – see community

feet, 17, **9:6, 9:8–9, 9:12–13, 9:38**, 123, 126, 157, 159
flagellation, **13:11**, 122
Flanders, 4–7, 9n, 18; see also Belgium
flour, miracle of, **12:26**
Fontevrault, 2
food, **8:8, 13:10, 15:20**, 117–18, 121, 124 and n, 125 and n, 137; see also eating
Fourth Lateran Council, 6
Fouque de Ramatuelle, **12:3**
fragrance, **3:10, 9:29, 14:17, 16:21, 16:26**, 158
France, 6, 7, 9, 10, 11, 12, 13, 18n, 141 and n, 146, 148–49; see also Gascony, Languedoc, Provence
Francis – see St. Francis
Franciscans (Friars Minor), 3–4, 7n, 8 and n, 11–15, 18n, 20, **1:2, 4:9–10, 4:14, 5:5, 6:8, 9:7, 9:9, 9:12, 9:15, 9:29–32, 9:34, 9:36–37, 9:43, 9:67–70, 10:3, 10:15, 10:17**, 71n, **10:35, 11:1–2, 11:12, 12:22, 13:5, 13:12–22, 14:3, 14:5, 14:25, 14:31, 14:34–36, 15:35–36, 15:38–39**, 120, 125 and n, 129, 130n, 132, 133, 135, 137, 141–42, 143–45, 146n, 147–48, 149 and n, 150 and n, 151–52, 156 and n, 157n; see also Conventuals, Spirituals
Franciscan Sisters, **2:7**, 145; see also Poor Clares
Frederick II, 22n
Friars Minor – see Franciscans
Free Spirit (heretical movement), 10; see also Beguine heresy

Gascony, 13
Genoa, **2:7**, 142, 145
Gerard of Borgo San Donnino, 12, 143n
Germany, 1, 6; see also Rhineland, Cologne
Gignac, Mabilia, **9:54**
Gignac, Raimond, **9:54**
golden ladder – see ladder of gold
Good Friday – see Holy Friday
Grace (God's), 19, **3:4–5, 4:13, 6:10, 9:17, 10:3, 10:10, 10:35, 12:4,**

12:18, 15:7, 15:31, 117, 127, 138, 140, 152
Gregorian reform, 1
Gregory IX (Pope), 6n
Grosseteste, Robert, 11
Guillaume de la Font, **14:4**
Guillaume Porcellet, 16

habit (of the Ladies of Roubaud), **2:5–9, 3:8, 4:11, 5:9, 11:13, 14:13**, 96n, **14:28–31**, 123, 129, 141, 150, 152–53
Hadewich of Brabant, 9n
hair shirt, **1:10, 1:13**, 28n, 121, 122n
headaches (of Douceline), **6:15, 9:59**, 123; see also illness, suffering
heresy, 7, 8, 10, 12, 15, 120, 124, 147; see also Albigensians, Beguine heresy, Cathars, Free Spirit
Heresy of the Free Spirit – see Free Spirit
Hildegard of Bingen, 1
Holy Friday (Good Friday), **9:48–50, 9:57, 10:27–28**, 131, 133
Holy Saturday, **10:29**, 133
Holy Thursday, **10:26–28, 12:8**, 133, 134, 140
Honorius III (Pope), 6
Honorius IV (Pope), 144
horse, cure of, **12:3**
host (Eucharist), **10:13–15**, 117, 118 and n, 124n, 129, 130 and n; see also Communion
Hugh de Digne (Douceline's brother), 7, 9, 11–13, 21, **1:2**, 25n, **2:7, 2:8–10, 3:1–4, 3:10, 4:12, 5:3, 5:11, 9:3, 10:3, 10:16, 10:33, 10:36–37, 13:22, 14:33–4, 15:6**, 114n, 125, 131n, 133–34, 141n, 142, 143–44, 145 and n, 146–48, 149–50, 151 and n, 156n, 157
Hugue de Digne (Douceline's mother), 7, **1:1, 1:4**
Huguette Blanche, **12:4**
Huguette de Fos, **9:73**, 157
Humiliati, 4
humility, 20, **2:4, 3:3–4, 10:32–34, 14:28–29, 16:32**, 116, 133, 143; humility of D: 21, **1:5, 4:1–9, 4:11–12, 4:14, 5:3, 5:6–7, 5:9, 6:11,**

9 780859 916295

CPSIA information can be obtained at www.ICGtesting.com
Printed in the USA
LVOW04s0724181214

419392LV00005B/23/P